Jubilees

Jubilees

The Hermeneia Translation

James C. VanderKam

Fortress Press
Minneapolis

JUBILEES
The Hermeneia Translation

Copyright © 2020 Fortress Press, an imprint of 1517 Media. All rights reserved. Except for brief quotations in critical articles or reviews, no part of this book may be reproduced in any manner without prior written permission from the publisher. Email copyright@1517.media or write to Permissions, Fortress Press, PO Box 1209, Minneapolis, MN 55440-1209.

Cover design: Kristin Miller
Interior design: The HK Scriptorium

Print ISBN: 978-1-5064-6703-0
eBook ISBN: 978-1-5064-6704-7

Contents

Preface   vii

Abbreviations and Sigla   ix

Introduction   1
   Contents of the Book of Jubilees   1
   Themes of the Book of Jubilees   2
   Translation   4
   Bibliography   5

Translation of the Book of Jubilees   7

Preface

The book of Jubilees is a narrative work by a Jewish author who composed it in Hebrew around the middle of the second century BCE. In it he reframed and rewrote the book of Genesis and the first parts of the book of Exodus. His second edition, as it were, of the stories from creation to Sinai has the distinction of being the oldest sustained commentary on the Genesis–Exodus narratives. It was probably written before there was a separated community of the Dead Sea Scrolls, but it was influential for that group and eventually for some other Jewish and Christian writers.

The translation of Jubilees that appears in the present book is the one found in my *Jubilees: A Commentary in Two Volumes* (Hermeneia; Minneapolis: Fortress, 2018). That translation is, in turn, a revision and updating of the one I published in *The Book of Jubilees* (2 vols., Corpus Scriptorum Christianorum Orientalium 510–11, Scriptores Aethiopici 87–88; Louvain: Peters, 1989), vol. 2. Most of the Hebrew fragments of Jubilees from the Qumran caves were published after the appearance of the 1989 volumes; the evidence from those copies was incorporated into the translation in the 2018 commentary. The only changes to the translation in the commentary that I have introduced here—and there are very few of them—involve matters of punctuation, apart from replacing one word in 39:10 (*bolt* instead of *door*) and altering some paragraphing to accommodate insertion of titles for each chapter and subheadings within the chapters. (In the two-volume commentary itself, the subheadings appear in the commentary proper, not in the translation.) A couple of subheadings in chapter 32 were also changed. The textual notes in the present volume, which were purposely kept to a minimum, are a small selection from and rewriting of ones in the commentary. They draw attention to noteworthy differences between the early witnesses and offer brief explanations of problems in the text.

I wish to express thanks to the editorial board of Hermeneia—A Critical and Historical Commentary on the Bible for permission to publish the translation in this format. I am grateful to Sidnie White Crawford, a board member, for encouraging the project and to Fortress Press, especially Will Bergkamp, for the invitation to prepare the volume. It has again been a great pleasure to profit from the skilled work of Maurya Horgan and Paul Kobelski of The HK Scriptorium in the preparation of the book.

James C. VanderKam
The University of Notre Dame

Abbreviations and Sigla

Abbreviations

chap.	chapter
Eth	Ethiopic
frg(s).	fragment(s)
Heb	Hebrew
Lat	Latin translation of Jubilees
lit.	literally
LXX	the Septuagint
ms(s)	manuscript(s)
MT	the Masoretic Text
n(s).	note(s)
OL	Old Latin translation of the Bible
pl.	plural
sing.	singular
SP	the Samaritan Pentateuch
Syr	Syriac
v(v)	verse(s)
vol(s).	volume(s)

Symbols in the Translation

( ) The enclosed words are added for a smoother English translation.

[ ] The enclosed words are probably part of the text but are missing from the textual witness(es); brackets surrounding a blank space indicate that a Hebrew fragment has room for more text but that the text is not preserved. Brackets also surround dates from creation, the equivalents of the year dates that Jubilees expresses in its system of jubilee periods, weeks, and years.

italics	The word or expression is an emendation.
underlining	The letters/words underlined are preserved on a Hebrew fragment.
{{ }}	The enclosed words are preserved on a Hebrew fragment but are of uncertain textual status (only in 2:19).

Introduction

Contents of the Book of Jubilees

The fifty-chapter book is divided formally into two unequal parts, chapter 1 and chapters 2–50. The first chapter supplies the setting for what follows. The author chose the scene at Mount Sinai described in Exodus 24 as the occasion when, on the sixteenth day of the third month, God and Moses conversed and God arranged for the book of Jubilees to be revealed. The Lord predicts in the opening chapter that Israel will soon violate the laws of the covenant made the previous day and will eventually suffer heavy punishments culminating in exile. In the future, however, a proper relationship will be restored, when the Lord, living among them in a new sanctuary, will be their God and they will be his righteous people. Moses objected, asking that God give his people a pure heart to obey him now, but the deity insisted that history would have to run its preordained course. Although the Lord speaks directly with Moses in chapter 1, at its end he orders an Angel of the (divine) Presence to dictate to Moses from heavenly tablets the contents of the book—the rewriting of Genesis and, more briefly, the first half of Exodus.

In chapters 2–50, the angel relates to Moses the story from creation (Genesis 1–2) until Israel's arrival at Mount Sinai (Exodus 19). The writer at times omits material from the older books, for example, the long story in Genesis 24 about getting a wife for Isaac (the sixty-seven-verse chapter in Genesis is summarized in one verse, Jub 19:10), and at other times adds sections (examples are accounts of wars fought against enemies by Jacob and his sons in Jub 34:1–9 and chaps. 37–38). He follows the general story line in Genesis and Exodus but along the way introduces many changes that serve his purposes.

1

Themes of the Book of Jubilees

Some of the more important points that the author makes as he rewrites the older stories are these.

1. God, the almighty Creator, fashioned a world that operates according to definite laws (chap. 2). This is true of natural phenomena over which God placed angels with specialized areas of supervision. The sun regulates a fixed year lasting 364 days; among them some days are holy, that is, for the Sabbaths and festivals (chap. 6). These years of unchanging length are basic building blocks in a chronology whose larger units are weeks of years (seven years) and jubilees (forty-nine years) by means of which the writer dates many events. It begins with creation and places the Israelite exodus from Egypt in the year of the world 2410 and the arrival at the border of Canaan in the year 2450, at the end of exactly fifty jubilee periods. At that time, Israel would rightfully enter the land assigned to their ancestor Shem, Noah's son, and later stolen by Canaan, a grandson of Noah (chaps. 8 and 10).

2. The one God, from the beginning, entered into a special relationship with the ancestors and thus with Israel, their descendants. God, the angels, and Israel observe the Sabbath (chap. 2) and jointly celebrate sacred festivals such as the one associated with the covenant, the Festival of Weeks (6:18). Circumcision was a rite ordained by God for Abraham and his descendants; Israelite males, like the two highest classes of angels—the angels of the presence and the angels of holiness—are to be circumcised (15:25-34). Israel, God's firstborn son, was not to mingle with the nations, all of which worshiped idols, but was to remain separate from them, with no intermarriage between them. God did not reveal the law to his people all at once; rather, he began disclosing it to the first generations and gradually supplemented it over the ensuing ones. That growing body of legislation, communicated to and transmitted by an unbroken line of priests from Adam to Levi, was at the heart of the one covenant that God established with Noah and his descendants, which was renewed annually with Abraham, Isaac, Jacob, and Israel. Starting with Enoch, the inventor of writing (4:17), that legal tradition took on written form. The pact at Sinai was only the latest in a series of renewals of the everlasting covenant. The entire law was inscribed on the heavenly tablets and thus was fixed.

3. God determined the course of history from the beginning. Events will take place as he determined, but the Lord's relationship with his people will not end. Eventually, after the nations, who were divinely subjected to the evil spirits (15:31), punish Israel, they will be destroyed and an obedient Israel will rule (chap. 23). The dead will not rise, but their spirits will rejoice at the great peace on earth that the living will experience. On the writer's view, the eschatological age had already begun in his time.

4. The writer based his account on Genesis and Exodus, but he was anxious that his Jewish contemporaries not misunderstand the older stories about Israel's ancestors. So, for example, it appears from Genesis that God revealed almost no laws to the patriarchs, apart from Sabbath (possibly; see Gen 2:1–3), the prohibition against consuming blood (9:4–6), and circumcision (Genesis 17); but, in Jubilees, Enoch, Noah, Abraham, Isaac, Jacob, and Moses were the recipients of laws and lived in accordance with them. They were also at times the human inaugurators of practices (e.g., festivals) revealed by God/the angels. Already to the ancients the Lord had disclosed Sabbath and circumcision, but he also revealed to them the sacred festivals (Weeks [6:17–22], Tabernacles [16:20–31]) and several other important laws, for example, sacrificial prescriptions (chap. 21) and the ban on intermarriage with other peoples (e.g., chaps. 22 and 30). In places where Genesis presents an ancestor in an unfavorable way, as, for instance, when Abram claimed that Sarai was his sister (Gen 12:13), the writer of Jubilees, as part of his effort to burnish their reputations, omits the embarrassing statement (see Jub 13:13–15). Or when Jacob deceived his father into blessing him by claiming to be his older son Esau (Genesis 27), the author has Jacob admit only to being Isaac's son and attributes Isaac's confusion to divine leading (Jub 26:18, 19). For the author, Rebekah had acted properly to ensure that the blessing would be given to the correct son, not to the reprehensible Esau. The writer wanted to prove that the genealogical line leading from the patriarchs to Israel was pure, so he was careful to identify by name the wives married by the patriarchs and their family connections. He also emphasized that, though some of Jacob's sons married outside the chosen line, the mistake was soon remedied (compare Gen 46:10, where Simeon is married to a Canaanite woman, with Jub 34:20, 21).

Translation

The translation presented here rests on the early textual evidence for the book of Jubilees. The following are the witnesses to the text of the book in the various languages in which such material survives. For a fuller discussion of the sources, see VanderKam, *Jubilees 1–21*, 1–16.

First, the book was composed in Hebrew. No complete or even nearly complete copy of it in this language has survived, but fragmentary remains of fourteen manuscripts have been identified among the Dead Sea Scrolls: 1Q17 and 18, 2Q19 and 20; 3Q5; 4Q216–224, 4Q176 frgs. 19–21; 11Q12. Among these copies, the oldest is 4Q216; it dates from approximately 125–100 BCE. The readings from the Hebrew manuscripts are indicated by underlining in the translation.

Second, the book was translated into Greek. No copy of the translation is available, but it was quoted by several Christian authors (e.g., Bishop Epiphanius and the Byzantine historian Syncellus) and served as a basis for later translations.

Third, it is possible, though perhaps not very likely, that a Hebrew text of the book was translated into Syriac. If there was a full Syriac translation, it was more likely made from a Greek base text. No complete Syriac translation has survived, but sections of Jubilees in Syriac are cited in a world chronicle that ends with the year 1234 CE. There is also a Syriac text that lists the names of the patriarchs' wives as found in Jubilees.

Fourth, a translation was made from Greek into Latin. One partial copy of that translation, dating to the fifth or sixth century CE, is available.

Fifth, a translation was made from Greek into Ge'ez, the classical language of Ethiopia. Jubilees was regarded as a scriptural book in the Ethiopian (Abyssinian) Church and was thus preserved in many copies. Almost fifty are known today, with the oldest dating to the fourteenth century CE. The Ethiopic version is the only one that offers the complete text of the book, so the English translation is necessarily based on it alone in many places, but where possible the textual evidence from the Ethiopic manuscripts is supplemented by the information from the remains of the versions listed above.

Bibliography

If a book or article in the list below is referred to in the textual notes, it is indicated by the author's name and the short title listed below at the end of the bibliographical entry for that author. The exception is the Hermeneia commentary on Jubilees; its two volumes are referenced by the short title alone, without the author's name.

Berger, Klaus. *Das Buch der Jubiläen* (JSHRZ 2.3; Gütersloh: Gütersloher Verlagshaus [Gerd Mohn], 1981). *Jubiläen*

Ceriani, Antonio Maria. *Monumenta Sacra et Profana* (2 vols.; Milan: Bibliotheca Ambrosiana, 1861–63).

Charles, R. H. *The Book of Jubilees or the Little Genesis* (London: Adam & Charles Black, 1902). *Jubilees*

———. *Maṣḥafa Kufālē or the Ethiopic Version of the Hebrew Book of Jubilees* (Anecdota Oxoniensia; Oxford: Clarendon, 1895). *Ethiopic Version*

Davenport, Gene L. *The Eschatology of the Book of Jubilees* (StPB 20; Leiden: Brill, 1971).

Dillmann, August. "Das Buch der Jubiläen oder die kleine Genesis," *Jahrbücher der Biblischen Wissenschaft* 2 (1850) 230–56; 3 (1851) 1–96. "Jubiläen"

Halpern-Amaru, Betsy. *The Empowerment of Women in the Book of Jubilees* (JSJSup 60; Leiden: Brill, 1999).

Hanneken, Todd. *The Subversion of the Apocalypses in the Book of Jubilees* (SBLEJL 34; Atlanta: Society of Biblical Literature, 2012).

Kugel, James L. *A Walk through Jubilees: Studies in the Book of Jubilees and the World of Its Creation* (JSJSup 156; Leiden: Brill, 2012).

Leslau, Wolf. *Comparative Dictionary of Geʿez* (Classical Ethiopic) (Wiesbaden: Harrassowitz, 1991). *Comparative Dictionary*

Petit, Françoise. *La chaîne sur la Genèse: Édition integrale I–IV* (Traditio Exegetica Graeca 1–4 (Louvain: Peeters, 1992–96). *La chaîne*

Ruiten, Jacques T. A. G. M van. *Abraham in the Book of Jubilees: The Rewriting of Genesis 11:26–25:10 in the Book of Jubilees 11:14–23:8* (JSJSup 161; Leiden: Brill, 2012).

———. *Primaeval History Interpreted: The Rewriting of Genesis 1–11 in the Book of Jubilees* (JSJSup 66; Leiden: Brill, 2000).

Scott, James. *On Earth as in Heaven: The Restoration of Sacred Time and Sacred Space in the Book of Jubilees* (JSJSup 91; Leiden: Brill, 2005).

Segal, Michael. *The Book of Jubilees: Rewritten Bible, Redaction, Ideology and Theology* (JSJSup 117; Leiden: Brill, 2007).

Testuz, Michel. *Les idées religieuses du Livre des Jubilés* (Geneva: Librairie E. Droz; Paris: Librairie Minard, 1960).

Tisserant, Eugène. "Fragments syriaques du Livre des Jubilés," *RB* 30 (1921) 55–86; 206–32.

VanderKam, James C. *The Book of Jubilees* (2 vols.; CSCO 510–11; Scriptores Aethiopici 87–88; Louvain: Peeters, 1989). *Book of Jubilees*

———. *The Book of Jubilees* (Guides to Apocrypha and Pseudepigrapha; Sheffield: Sheffield Academic Press, 2001).

———. *Jubilees: A Commentary in Two Volumes* (Hermeneia; Minneapolis: Fortress Press, 2018). *Jubilees 1–21* and *Jubilees 22–50*

VanderKam, James C., and J. T. Milik. "Jubilees," in James C. VanderKam, consulting ed., *Qumran Cave IV.VIII: Parabiblical Texts, Part 1* (DJD 13; Oxford: Clarendon, 1994) 1–185. DJD 13

Werman, Cana. *The Book of Jubilees: Introduction, Translation, and Interpretation* (Between Bible and Mishnah; Jerusalem: Yiṣḥaq ben-Zvi, 2015 [Hebrew]). *Jubilees*

Translation of the Book of Jubilees

Prologue

These are the words regarding the divisions of the times for the law and for the testimony, for the events of the years, for the weeks of their jubilees throughout all the years of eternity as he related (them) to Moses on Mount Sinai when he went up to re<u>c</u>eive the stone tablets—the law and the commandment—<u>by the word of the Lord</u> as he had told him that he should come up <u>to the summit of the mou</u>ntain.

The Setting and Purpose of the Book (Chapter 1)

Narrative Setting (1:1–4)

1:1/   During the first year of the Israelites' exodus from Egypt, in <u>the third mon</u>th—on the sixteenth of <u>this</u> month—<u>the Lord said to</u> Moses: "Come up to me to <u>the mountain</u>. I will give you the two <u>stone</u> tablets, <u>the law</u> and the commandment that I have written so that you may <u>tea</u>ch them." 2/ So Moses went up the mountain of the Lord. The <u>glory of the Lord</u> took up residence on Mount Sinai, and a cloud covered it for six days. 3/ When he summoned Moses into the cloud on the seventh day, he saw the glory of the Lord like a fire blazing on the summit of the mountain. 4/ Moses remained on the mountain for 40 days and 40 nights while the Lord showed him what (had happened) beforehand as well as what was to come. He related to him the d<u>i</u>v<u>i</u>sions of the t<u>i</u>mes <u>for the law</u> and for the testimony.

Conversation between the Lord and Moses (1:5–26)

The Lord's First Speech (1:5–18)

5/ He said to him: "Pay attention to all the words that I tell you on this mountain. Write them in a book so that their generations may know that I have not abandoned them because of all the evil they have done in *breaking*[a] the covenant between me and your children that I am making today on Mount Sinai for their offspring. 6/ So it will be that when all of these things befall them they will recognize that I have been more faithful than they in all their judgments and in all their curses.[b] They will recognize that I have indeed been with them.

7/ "Now you write this entire message that I am telling you today, because I know their defiance and their stubbornness (even) before I bring them into the land that I promised by oath to their ancestors Abraham, Isaac, and Jacob: 'To your posterity I will give the land that flows with milk and honey'. When they eat and are full, 8/ they will turn after other[c] gods who will not save them from any afflictions. Then the testimony is to correspond[d] with this testimony. 9/ For they will forget all my commandments—everything that I command you—and will follow the nations, their idols, and their abominations. They will serve their gods, and (this) will prove an obstacle for them—an affliction, a pain, and a trap. 10/ Many will be destroyed. They will be captured and will fall into the enemy's control because they abandoned my statutes, my commandments, my covenantal festivals, my Sabbaths, my holy things which they have hallowed for me among them, my tabernacle, and my temple that I sanctified for myself in the

---

a Although the mss read a verb meaning *lead astray, corrupt*, the context shows that a word meaning *break* is required, as in Deut 31:20.

b The Eth mss read *actions*, but 4Q216 i:16 very likely has *curses*.

c The Eth mss read *foreign*, but 4Q216 ii:4 has *other* (see LXX Deut 31:20; LXX Josh 24:20).

d Most mss read *testify*, but 4Q216 ii:4 has *answer*. Deuteronomy 31:21 lies behind the passage. *Correspond* is an attempt to express the sense of *answer* in the context.

middle of the land so that I could set my name on it and that it could live (there). 11/ They will make for themselves high places, (sacred) groves, and carved images; they will bow to all the works of their error. They will sacrifice their children to demons and to every product (conceived by) their erring minds. 12/ I will send witnesses to them so that I may testify to them, but they will not listen and will kill the witnesses. They will persecute those too who study the law. They will neglect everything and will begin to do evil in my presence. 13 Then I will hide my face from them. I will deliver them into the control of the nations for captivity, for devastation, and for devouring. I will remove them from the land and disperse them among all the nations. 14/ They will forget all my laws, all my commandments, and all my verdicts. They will forget beginning(s) of the month, Sabbath, festival, jubilee, and covenant.

15/ "After this they will return to me from among the nations with all their minds, all their souls, and all their strength. Then I will gather them from among all the nations, and they will search for me so that I may be found by them when they have searched for me with all their minds and with all their souls. I will rightly disclose to them abundant peace. 16/ I will *plant* them[a] as a righteous plant with all my mind and with all my soul. They will become a blessing, not a curse; they will become the head, not the tail. 17/ I will build my temple among them and will live with them; I will be their God and they will be my true and righteous people. 18/ I will neither abandon them nor become alienated from them, for I am the Lord their God."

---

a The Eth mss read *I will banish/change them*, which seems inappropriate in a context offering promises. R. H. Charles (*Jubilees*, 5) probably found the correct answer for the wrong verb: two Heb words that resemble each other were confused, *nsʿ* (*travel*, causative: *make travel*) and *ntʿ* (*plant*).

Moses's Intercession for the Nation (1:19–21)

19/ Then Moses fell prostrate and prayed and said: "Lord my God, do not allow your people and your heritage to go along in the error of their minds, and do not deliver them into the control of the nations with the result that they rule over them lest they make them sin against you. 20/ May your mercy, Lord, be lifted over your people. Create for them a just spirit. May the spirit of Belial not rule over them so as to bring charges against them before you and to make them stumble away from every proper path so that they may be destroyed from your presence. 21/ They are your people and your heritage whom you have rescued from Egyptian control by your great power. Create for them a pure mind and a holy spirit. May they not be trapped in their sins from now to eternity."

The Lord's Second Speech (1:22–26)

22/ Then the Lord said to Moses: "I know their contrary nature, their way of thinking, and their stubbornness. They will not listen until they acknowledge their sins and the sins of their ancestors. 23/ After this they will return to me in a fully upright manner and with all (their) minds and all (their) souls. I will cut away the foreskins of their minds and the foreskins of their descendants' minds. I will create a holy spirit for them and will purify them in order that they may not turn away from me from that time forever. 24/ Their souls will adhere to me and to all my commandments. They will perform my commandments. I will be their Father and they will be my children. 25/ All of them will be called children of the living God. Every angel and every spirit will know them. They will know that they are my children and that I am their Father in a just and proper way and that I love them.

26/ "Now you write all these words that I tell you on this mountain: what is first and what is <u>last</u> and what is to come during all the divisions of the times that are for the la<u>w</u> and <u>for the testim</u>ony and for the weeks of their jubilees until eternity—until the time when I descend <u>and live wi</u>th them throughout all the ages of eternity."

Narrative Note about the Angel and Divine Words about the Future (1:27–28)

27/ Then he told the Angel of the <u>Presence to dictate</u> to Moses[a] (starting) from the beginning of the creation unti<u>l the time when "my temple is built</u> among them throughout the ages of eternity. 28/ The Lord will appear in the sight of <u>all</u>, and all <u>will know</u> that I am the God of Israel, the Father of all <u>Jacob's</u> children, <u>and King</u> on Mount Zion for the ages of eternity. Then Zion and Jerusa<u>l</u>em will be holy."

Narrative Note about the Revelation and Its Scope (1:29)

29/ The Angel of the Presence, who was going along in front of the Israelite camp, took the tablets (that told) of the divisions of the years from the time the law and the testimony were created—for the weeks of their jubilees, year by year in their full number, and their jubilees from [the time of the first creation until][b] the time of the new creation when the heavens, the earth, and all their creatures will be renewed like the powers of the sky and like all the creatures of the earth, until the time when the temple of the Lord will be created in Jerusalem on Mount Zion. All the luminaries will be renewed for (the purpose of) healing, health, and blessing for all the elect ones of Israel and so that it may remain this way from that time throughout all the days of the earth.

---

a The verb *dictate* is very likely the reading in 4Q216 iv:6. At this place the Eth mss have *write*. The explanation for the difference is that the Eth reading assumes the verb is the simple form *write*, whereas the Heb shows the form is causative, *cause to write/dictate*. By reading *write* in this passage the Eth mss introduce a contradiction into the book, since Moses, not the angel, is listed as the writer of Jubilees in other places (1:5, 7, 26; 2:1; 23:32; 33:18).

b The Eth text reads *from the time of the new creation*, but the context suggests something like the bracketed words have been omitted (M. Stone, "Apocryphal Notes and Readings," *Israel Oriental Studies* 1 [1971] 125–26).

The Creation, the Sabbath, and Israel (Chapter 2)

The Six Days of Creation (2:1–16)

2:1/ On the Lord's orders the Angel of the Presence said to Moses, Write all the words about the creation—how on the sixth day the Lord God completed all his works, everything that he had created, and kept Sabbath on the seventh day. He sanctified it for all ages and set it as a sign for all his works. 2/ For on the first day he created the heavens that are above, the earth, the waters, and all the spirits who serve before him, namely, the angels of the presence; the angels of holiness; the angels of the spirits of fire; the angels of the winds that blow; the angels of the spirits of the clouds for darkness, ice, hoarfrost, dew,[a] snow,[b] hail, and frost; the angels of the thunder; and for the angels of the winds [   ];[c] and the angels of the spirits for cold and heat, for winter and summer, and for all the spirits of his creatures that [he made] in the heavens and that (he made) on the earth,[d] and in every (place). [There were also] the depths, darkness and dawn, light and evening that he prepared through his knowledge. 3/ Then we saw his works and blessed him regarding all his works; we offered praise before him because he had made seven great works on the first day.

---

  a The nouns *ice, hoar-frost, dew* are not present here in the Eth copies. They have been placed in the translation because 4Q216 v:7 would be too short without several extra terms. Epiphanius, when speaking about day 1, lists these terms among the items that came from the water. Milik (DJD 13:15) suggested they be read here.

  b Most Eth mss read *all*, while others omit the word. Epiphanius, however, uses the more appropriate *snow* here; the Greek for *snow—chionos*—may have been miscopied as *pantos* (Charles, *Jubilees*, 13).

  c The brackets enclosing an empty space represent the fact that there is room on 4Q216 v:8 for additional material here, but what it was is not known because the other versions supply no readings at this point. See *Jubilees 1–21*, 169, for a fuller discussion.

  d Retroverting the Eth reading *and what is in the heavens and what is on the earth* (all words but the first *and* are in Epiphanius's version) would be too short for the amount of space available on 4Q216 v:9. For that reason *he made* has been supplied twice.

4/ On the second day he made a firmament between the waters, and the waters were divided on that day. Half of them went up above the firmament and half of them went down below the firmament (which was) in the middle above the surface of the whole earth. This was the only work that he made on the second day.

5/ On the third day he did as he said to the waters that they should pass from the surface of the whole earth to one place and that the dry land should appear. 6/ The waters did so, as he told them. They withdrew from the surface of the earth to one place apart from this firmament, and dry land appeared. 7/ On that day he created for it all the seas—each with the places where they collected—all the rivers, and the places where the waters collected in the mountains and on the whole earth; all the reservoirs, all the dew of the earth; the seed that is sown—with each of its kinds—all that *sprouts*,[a] the fruit trees, the forests, and the Garden of Eden (which is) in Eden for enjoyment and for *food*.[b] These four great types he made on the third day.

8/ On the fourth day the Lord made the sun, the moon, and the stars. He placed them in the heavenly firmament to shine on the whole earth, to rule over day and night, and to separate between light and darkness. 9/ The Lord appointed the sun as a great sign above the earth for days, Sabbaths, months, festivals, years, Sabbaths of years, jubilees, and all cycles of the years. 10/ It separates between light and darkness and (serves) for well-being so that everything that sprouts and grows on the earth may prosper. These three types he made on the fourth day.

11/ On the fifth day he created the great sea monsters within the watery depths, for these were the first fleshly products of his hands; all the fish that move about in the waters, all flying birds, and all their kinds. 12/ The sun shone over them

---

a The Eth mss read *what is eaten*, while Epiphanius has *things that sprout/grow*. A confusion of similar Eth verbs probably caused the wrong reading in Eth.

b The reading in the Eth mss is *for all*. It is likely that Heb *l'kl* (*for food* [as in Gen 2:9]) was misread as *lkl* (*for all*) to produce the Eth text.

for (their) <u>well-being and over</u> everything <u>that was on the</u> <u>e</u>arth—all that sprouts from the ground, all fruit trees, and all animate beings. These <u>three great</u>[a] <u>kinds</u> he made on the fifth day.

13/ On <u>the sixth day</u> he made <u>all</u> the <u>land animals</u>, all cattle, and everything that moves about on the earth. 14/ After all this, <u>he made humankind—a male and a fem</u>ale he made them. He made him rule everything on earth and in the seas and over flying creatures, <u>animals, everything that moves</u> about on the earth, cattle, and the entire earth. Over all these he made him rule. <u>These</u> four <u>kinds he made on the</u> sixth day.

15/ The total was 22 kinds. 16/ He finished all his works on the sixth day: everything <u>in heaven, on the earth</u>, in the seas, in the depths, in the light, in the darkness, and in every (place).

Sabbath and Israel (2:17–33)

17/ He gave us as a great sign <u>the Sabbath day on</u> which <u>he rested</u> [   ][b] so that work should <u>be done</u> for six days [   ][c] <u>and that we should keep Sabbath</u> from all work <u>on the seventh day</u>. 18/ <u>He told</u> us—all the angels of the presence and all the angels of holiness, <u>these</u> two <u>kinds</u>—to keep Sabbath with him in heaven and on earth.

19/ He said to us: "I will now separate <u>a people</u> for myself <u>among my nations</u>. They, too, will keep Sabbath. I will sanctify a people for myself and will bless them {{as I sanctified the Sabbath day. I will sanctify them for myself; in this way I will bless them.}}[d] They will be my people and I will be

---

a The Eth mss lack *great*, but traces of the Heb word for *great/large* are legible on 4Q216 vi:14.

b 4Q216 vii:6–7 would have had space for considerably more text than a retroversion of the Eth readings would supply. There is no clear evidence, however, for what the extra words would have been, other than that they would have dealt with the Sabbath.

c The Heb fragment again has more space than the wording at this point in the versions supplies (*Jubilees 1–21*, 171).

d The words are enclosed in double braces because it is not clear that they belong in the text. They are present in Eth mss, but there is insufficient space for them in 4Q216 vii:10, which may be shorter due to omission caused by a scribe's eye jumping from *I will bless them* before the words in question to *I will bless them* at their end.

their God. 20/ I have chosen[a] the descendants of Jacob as a treasured[b] people from all the nations. I have recorded them as my firstborn son and have sanctified them for myself throughout the ages of eternity. I will tell them about the seventh day so that they may keep Sabbath from all work on it." 21/ In this way he made a sign on it by which they, too, would keep Sabbath with us on the seventh day to eat, drink, and bless the Creator of all[c] as he had blessed them and sanctified them for himself as a treasured people out of all the nations; and to be keeping Sabbath together with us. 22/ He made his commands rise as a fine fragrance that is to be acceptable in his presence for all times.

23/ There were 22 leaders of humanity from Adam until him; and 22 kinds of works were made until the seventh day. The latter is blessed and holy and the former, too, is blessed and holy. Both were made together for holiness and blessing. 24/ It was granted to these that for all times they should be the blessed and holy ones. This is the testimony and the first law, as it was sanctified and blessed on the seventh day. 25/ He created the heavens, the earth, and everything that was created in six days. The Lord gave a holy festal day to all his creation. For this reason he gave orders regarding it that anyone who would do any work on it was to die; also, the one who would defile it was to die.

26/ Now you command the Israelites to observe this day so that they may sanctify it, not do any work on it, and not defile it for it is holier than all (other) days. 27/ Anyone who profanes it is to die and anyone who does any work on it is to be cut off eternally so that the Israelites may observe this day throughout their history and not be cut off from the earth.

---

a 4Q216 vii:11 seems to have a mistaken reading. The context strongly favors a first-person sing. form here, but the fragment has *wbḥr: he chose*.

b The Eth mss have *za-re'iku: whom I have seen*, but the reading may be a mistaken translation for the common expression for Israel as God's special people, as in Deut 7:6; cf. Exod 19:5. The next verse contains a correct form for the expression: *za-yastare"i*.

c The scribe of 4Q216 vii:12 may have omitted the words from the beginning of the verse to this point, perhaps when he skipped from *all* near the end of v 20 to *all* here.

For it is a holy day; it is a blessed day. 28/ Everyone who observes (it) and keeps Sabbath on it from all his work will be holy and blessed throughout all times like us. 29/ Inform and tell the Israelites the law (that relates to) this day and that they should keep Sabbath on it and not neglect it through the error of their minds lest they do (any) work on it—(the day) on which it is not proper to do what they wish, namely, to prepare on it anything that is to be eaten or drunk; to draw water; to bring in or remove on it anything that one carries in their gates—(any) work that they had not prepared for themselves in their dwellings on the sixth day. 30/ They are not to bring (anything) out or in from house to house on this day because it is more holy and more blessed than any day of the jubilee of jubilees. On it we kept Sabbath in heaven before it was made known to all humanity that on it they should keep Sabbath on earth. 31/ The Creator of all blessed but did not sanctify any people(s) and nations to keep Sabbath on it except Israel alone. To it alone did he give (the right) to eat, drink, and keep Sabbath on it upon the earth. 32/ The Creator of all who created this day blessed it for (the purposes of) blessing, holiness, and glory more than all (other) days. 33/ This law and testimony were given to the Israelites as an eternal law throughout their history.

Life Outside, In, and Outside the Garden (Chapter 3)

Finding a Helper for Adam (3:1–7)

3:1/ During six days of the second week we brought to Adam, on the Lord's orders, all animals, all cattle, all birds, everything that moves about on the earth, and everything that moves about in the water—in their various kinds and various forms: the animals on the first day; the cattle on the second day; the birds on the third day; everything that moves about on the earth on the fourth day; and the ones that move about in the water on the fifth day. 2/ Adam named them all, each with its own name. Whatever he called them became their name. 3/ During these five days Adam was looking at all of these—male and female among every kind that was on the earth. But he himself was alone; there was no one whom he found for himself who would be for him a helper who was like him. 4/ Then the Lord said to us: "It is not good that the man should be alone. Let us make him a helper who is like him." 5/ The Lord our God imposed a sound slumber on him and he fell asleep. Then he took one of his bones for a woman. That rib was the origin of the woman—from among his bones. He built up the flesh in its place and built the woman. 6/ Then he awakened Adam from his sleep. When he awoke, he got up on the sixth day. Then he brought (him) to her.[a] He knew her and said to her: "This is now bone from my bone and flesh from my flesh. This one will be called my wife, for she was taken from her husband." 7/ For this reason a man and a woman are to become one, and for this reason he leaves his father and his mother. He associates with his wife, and they become one flesh.

Law for a Woman Who Gives Birth (3:8–14)

8/ In the first week Adam and his wife—the rib—were created, and in the second week he showed her to him. Therefore, a commandment was given to keep (women) in their defilement seven days for a male (child) and for a female two (units) of seven days. 9/ After 40 days had come to an end for Adam in the land where he had been created, we brought him into the Garden of Eden to work and keep it. His wife was brought (there) on the eightieth day. After this she entered the Garden of Eden. 10/ For this reason a commandment was written in the heavenly tablets for the one who gives birth to a child: if she gives birth to a male, she is to remain in her impurity for seven days like the first seven days; then for 33 days she is to remain in the blood of (her) purification. She is not to touch any sacred thing nor enter the sanctuary until she completes these days for a male. 11/ As for a female

---

[a] There is some variation among the Eth mss regarding who did the bringing, who was brought, and to whom, but the rendering above seems the best one.

she is to remain in her impurity for two weeks of days like the first two weeks and 66 days in the blood of (her) purification. Their total is 80 days. 12/ After she had completed these 80 days, we brought her into the Garden of Eden because it is the holiest in the entire earth, and every tree that is planted in it is holy. 13/ For this reason the law of these days has been ordained for the one who gives birth to a male or a female. She is not to touch any sacred thing nor enter the sanctuary until the time when those days for a male or a female are completed. 14/ These are the law and testimony that were written for Israel to keep for all times.

Seven Good Years (3:15–16)

15/ During the first week of the first jubilee Adam and his wife spent the seven years in the Garden of Eden working and guarding it. We gave him work and were teaching him (how) to do everything that was appropriate for working (it). 16/ While he was working (it) he was naked but did not realize (it) nor was he ashamed. He would guard the garden against birds, animals, and cattle. He would gather its fruit and eat (it) and would store its surplus for himself and his wife. He would store what was being kept.

Sin and Expulsion (3:17–35)

17/ When the conclusion of the seven years which he had completed there arrived—seven years exactly—in the second month, on the seventeenth, the serpent came and approached the woman. The serpent said to the woman: "Is it from all the fruit of the trees in the garden (that) the Lord has commanded you: 'Do not eat from it?'" 18/ She said to him: "From all the fruit of the tree(s) that are in the garden the Lord told us: 'Eat.' But from the fruit of the tree that is in the middle of the garden he told us: 'Do not eat from it and do not touch it so that you may not die.'" 19/ Then the serpent said to the woman: "You will not really die because the Lord knows that when you eat from it your eyes will be opened, you will become like gods, and you will know good and evil." 20/ The woman saw that the tree was delightful and pleasing to the eye and (that) its fruit was good to eat. So she took some of it and ate (it). 21/ She first covered her shame with fig leaves and then gave it to Adam. He ate (it), his eyes were opened, and he saw that he was naked. 22/ He took fig leaves and sewed (them); (thus) he made himself an apron and covered his shame.

23/ The Lord cursed the serpent and was angry at it forever. At the woman, too, he was angry because she had listened to the serpent and eaten. He said to her: 24/ "I will indeed multiply your sadness and your pain. Bear children in sadness. Your place of refuge will be with your husband; he will rule over you." 25/ Then he said to Adam: "Because you listened to your wife and ate from the tree from which I commanded you not to eat, may the ground be cursed on account of you. May it grow thorns and thistles for you. Eat your food in the sweat of your face until you return to the earth from which you were taken. For earth you are and to earth you will return."

26/ He made clothing out of skins for them, clothed them, and dismissed them from the Garden of Eden. 27/ On that day, as he was leaving the Garden of Eden, he burned incense as a pleasing fragrance—frankincense, galbanum, stacte, and aromatic spices—in the early morning when the sun rose at the time when he covered his shame. 28/ On that day the mouths of all the animals, the cattle, the birds, everything that walks and everything that moves about were made incapable of speaking because all of them used to converse with one another in one language and one tongue. 29/ He dismissed from the Garden of Eden all the animate beings that were in the Garden of Eden. All animate beings were dispersed—each by its kind and each by its nature—into the place(s) that had been created for them. 30/ But of all the animals and cattle he permitted Adam alone to cover his shame. 31/ For this reason it has been commanded in the tablets regarding all those who know the judgment of the law that they cover their shame and not uncover themselves as the nations uncover themselves.

32/ At the beginning of the fourth month Adam and his wife departed from the Garden of Eden. They lived in the land of Elda, in the land where they were created. 33/ Adam named his wife Eve. 34/ They were childless throughout[a] the first jubilee; afterwards he knew her. 35/ He himself was working the land as he had been taught in the Garden of Eden.

The First Generations (Chapter 4)

The First Family (4:1–6)

4:1/ In the third week in the second jubilee [years 64–70], she gave birth to Cain; in the fourth [71–77] she gave birth to Abel; and in the fifth [78–84] she gave birth to his daughter Awan. 2/ During the first (week) of the third jubilee [99–105] Cain killed Abel because we had accepted[b] his sacrifice from him but from Cain we had not accepted (one). 3/ When he killed him in a field, his blood cried out from the ground to heaven—crying because he had been killed. 4/ The Lord blamed Cain regarding Abel because he had killed him. While he allowed him a length (of time) on the earth because of his brother's blood, he cursed him upon the earth.

5/ For this reason it has been written on the heavenly tablets: "Cursed is the person who beats his companion maliciously." All who saw (it) said: "May it be. And let the man who has seen but has not told be cursed like him." 6/ For this reason we report, when we come before the Lord our God, all the sins that take place[c] in heaven and on earth—what (happens) in the light, in the darkness, or in any place.

---

a The Eth word *'eska* normally means *until*, but, as that makes little sense in the expression, it probably has another of its meanings here—*within/for* (Leslau, *Comparative Dictionary*, 42).

b Rather than *we had accepted*, some mss read *he had accepted*. The same variant occurs later in the verse at *we had not accepted*.

c 11QJub 1 2; the Eth mss read *are/take place* (*yekawwen*).

The Sethite Genealogy (4:7–33)

Generations 2–6 (4:7–16)

7/ Adam and his wife spent four weeks of years mourning for Abel. Then in the fourth year of the fifth week [130] they became happy. Adam again knew his wife, and she gave birth to a son for him. He named him Seth because he said, "The Lord has raised up for us another offspring on the earth in place of Abel" (for Cain had killed him). 8/ In the sixth week [134–140] he became the father of his daughter Azura. 9/ Cain married his sister Awan, and at the end of the fourth jubilee [148–196] she gave birth to Enoch for him. In the first year of the first week of the fifth jubilee [197] houses were built on the earth. Then Cain built a city and named it after his son Enoch. 10/ Adam knew his wife Eve, and she gave birth to nine more children. 11/ In the fifth week of the fifth jubilee [225–231] Seth married his sister Azura, and in its fourth (year) [235] she gave birth to Enosh for him. 12/ He was the first to call on the Lord's name on the earth. 13/ In the seventh jubilee, in the third week [309–315] Enosh married his sister Noam. She gave birth to a son for him in the third year of the fifth week [325], and he named him Kenan. 14/ At the end of the eighth jubilee [344–392] Kenan married his sister Mualelit. She gave birth to a son for him in the ninth jubilee, in the first week—in the third year of this week [395]—and he named him Malalael.

15/ During the second week of the tenth jubilee [449–455] Malalael married Dinah, the daughter of Barakiel, the daughter of his father's *brother*.[a] She gave birth to a son for him in the third week, in its sixth year [461]. He named him Jared because during his lifetime the angels of the Lord who were called Watchers descended to earth to teach humanity and to do what is just and upright upon the earth. 16/ In the

---

a The Eth mss read *father's sister*; the same happens in vv 16, 20, 27, 28, 33. It is likely that in the Greek translation of Jubilees the form *patradelphos* (*father's brother*) was used and that the translator into Ge'ez misunderstood it to mean *father's sister*. The Syr citation of this passage has the equivalent of *father's brother* (*Jubilees 1–21*, 248).

eleventh jubilee [491–539] Jared took a wife for himself, and her name was Barakah, the daughter of Rasu'eyal, the daughter of his father's *brother*, in the fourth week of this jubilee [512–518]. She gave birth to a son for him during the fifth week, in the fourth year, of the jubilee [522], and he named him Enoch.

Generation 7: Enoch (4:17–26)

17/ He was the first of humanity who were born on the earth who learned (the art of) writing, instruction, and wisdom and who wrote down in a book the signs of the sky in accord with the fixed patterns of their months so that humanity would know the seasons of the years according to the fixed patterns of each of their months. 18/ He was the first to write a testimony. He testified to humanity in the generations of the earth. The weeks of the jubilees he related, and made known the days of the years; the months he arranged, and related the sabbaths of the years, as we had told him. 19/ While he slept he saw in a vision what has happened and what will occur—how things will happen for humanity during their history until the day of judgment. He saw everything and understood. He wrote a testimony for himself and placed it upon the earth against all humanity and for their history.

20/ During the twelfth jubilee, in its seventh week [582–588] he took a wife for himself. Her name was Edni, the daughter of Daniel, the daughter of his father's *brother*. In the sixth year of this week [587] she gave birth to a son for him, and he named him Methuselah.

21/ He was, moreover, with God's angels for six jubilees of years. They showed him everything on earth and in the heavens—the dominion of the sun—and he wrote down everything. 22/ He testified to the Watchers who had sinned with the daughters of men because these had begun to mix with earthly women[a] so that they became defiled. Enoch testified against all of them.

---

a Lit., *the daughters of the earth* (*'adamah*). Other excellent copies read *the daughters of man/Adam* (*'adam*).

23/ He was taken from human society, and we led him into the Garden of Eden for (his) greatness and honor. Now he is there writing down the judgment and condemnation of the world and all the wickedness of humanity. 24/ Because of him the floodwater did not come[a] on any of the land of Eden because he was placed there as a sign and to testify against all people in order to tell all the deeds of history until the day of judgment. 25/ He burned the evening incense of the sanctuary that is acceptable before the Lord on the mountain of incense.[b] 26/ For there are four places on earth that belong to the Lord: the Garden of Eden, the mountain of the east, this mountain on which you are today—Mount Sinai—and Mount Zion (which) will be sanctified in the new creation for the sanctification of the earth. For this reason the earth will be sanctified from all its sins and from its uncleanness into the history of eternity.

Generations 8 and 9 (4:27–28)

27/ During this jubilee—that is, the fourteenth jubilee—Methuselah married Edna, the daughter of Ezrael, the daughter of his father's *brother*, in the third week in the first year of that *week*[c] [652]. He became the father of a son whom he named Lamech. 28/ In the fifteenth jubilee, in the third week [701–707], Lamech married a woman whose name was Betanosh, the daughter of Barakiel, the daughter of his father's *brother*. During this week she gave birth to a son for him, and he named him Noah, explaining: "*This one*[d] will give me consolation from my sadness, from all my work, and from the earth the Lord cursed."

---

a *Did not come* (*'i-maṣ'a*). Almost all of the Eth mss read a form that has a very similar appearance, *'amṣe'a* (*he brought*), which contradicts the sense of the passage.

b The best Eth mss read *qatr* (*midday, noon, midday heat*) which is unexpected. *Qatr* may be a miswriting of *qetāre* (*incense*). The Syr citation has *south*, also a term that does not fit the context, as Eden is in the east.

c The Eth mss read *year*, but the context requires *week*.

d Most Eth copies have *who* (*za-*), an easy mistake for *ze-* (*this* [*one-*]); see Gen 5:29.

Death of Adam (4:29–30)

29/ At the end of the nineteenth jubilee, during the seventh week—in its sixth year [930]—Adam died. All his children buried him in the land where he had been created. He was the first to be bu<u>ried in the</u> ground. 30/ He lacked 70 years from 1,000 years because <u>1,000</u> <u>ye</u>ars are[a] one day in the testimony of heaven. For this reason it was written regarding the tr<u>ee of knowledge:</u> "<u>On</u> the day that you eat from it you will die." Therefore he did not complete <u>the years of</u> this <u>day</u> because he died during it.

Death of Cain (4:31–32)

31/ At the conclusion of this jubilee Cain was killed <u>after him</u> in the same year. His house fell on him, and he died inside his house. He was killed by <u>its</u> stone<u>s for</u> with a stone he had killed Abel and, by a just punishment, he was killed with a stone. 32/ For this reason it has been ordained on the heavenly tablets: "By the instrument with which a man kills his fellow he is to be killed. As he wounded him so are they to do to him."

Generations 10 and 11: Noah and His Family (4:33)

33/ In the twenty-fifth jubilee Noah married a woman whose name was Emzara, the daughter of Barakiel, the daughter of his *father's brother*—during the first year in the fifth week [1205]. In its third year [1207] she gave birth to Shem for him; in its fifth year [1209] she gave birth to Ham for him; and in the first year during the sixth week [1212] she gave birth to Japheth for him.

Angels and Women, Judgment and Flood (Chapter 5)

The Growth of Evil on the Earth (5:1–5)

5:1/ When humanity began to multiply on the surface of the entire earth and daughters were born to them, the angels of the

---

a Some Eth mss add *like*.

Lord—in a certain (year) of this jubilee—saw that they were beautiful to look at. So they married of them whomever they chose. They gave birth to children for them and they were giants. 2/ Wickedness increased on the earth. All animate beings corrupted their way—(everyone of them) from people to cattle, animals, birds, and everything that moves about on the ground. All of them corrupted their way and their prescribed course. They began to devour one another, and wickedness increased on the earth. Every thought of all humanity's knowledge was evil like this all the time. 3/ The Lord saw that the earth was corrupt, (that) all animate beings had corrupted their prescribed course, and (that) all of them—everyone that was on the earth—had acted wickedly before his eyes. 4/ He said that he would obliterate people and all animate beings that were on the surface of the earth that he had created. 5/ He was pleased with Noah alone.

Punishments (5:6–12)

6/ Against his angels whom he had sent to the earth he was angry enough to uproot them from all their (positions of) authority. He told us to tie them up in the depths of the earth; now they are tied within them and are alone. 7/ Regarding their children there went out from his presence an order to strike them with the sword and to remove them from beneath the sky. 8/ He said, "My spirit will not remain on people forever for they are flesh. Their life span is to be 120 years." 9/ He sent his sword among them so that they would kill one another. They began to kill each other until all of them fell by the sword and were obliterated from the earth. 10/ Now their fathers were watching, but afterwards they were tied up in the depths of the earth until the great day of judgment when there will be condemnation on all who have corrupted their ways and their actions[a] before the Lord. 11/ He obliterated all from their places; there remained no one of them whom he did not judge for all their wickedness. 12/ He made a new

---

a For *action*, some mss read *plan*.

and righteous nature for all his creatures so that they would not sin with their whole nature until eternity. Everyone will be righteous—each according to his kind—for all time.

Justice for All (5:13–16)

13/ The judgment of them all has been ordained and written on the heavenly tablets; there is no injustice. (As for) all who transgress from their way in which it was ordained for them to go—if they do not go in it, judgment has been written down for each creature and for each kind. 14/ There is nothing that is in heaven or on the earth, in the light, the darkness, Sheol, the deep, or in the dark place—all their judgments have been ordained, written, and inscribed. 15/ He will exercise judgment regarding everyone—the great one in accord with his greatness and the small one in accord with his smallness—each one in accord with his way. 16/ He is not one who shows favoritism nor one who takes a bribe, if he says he will execute judgment against everyone. If someone gave everything on earth he would not show favoritism nor would he accept (it) from him because he is the righteous judge.

Exceptions (5:17–19)

17/ Regarding the Israelites it has been written and ordained: "If they turn to him in the right way, he will forgive all their wickedness and will pardon all their sins." 18/ It has been written and ordained that he will have mercy on all who turn[a] from all their errors once each year. 19/ To all who corrupted their ways and their plan(s) before the flood no favor was shown except to Noah alone because favor was shown to him for the sake of his children whom he saved from the floodwaters for his sake because his mind was righteous in all his ways, as it had been commanded concerning him. He did not transgress from anything that had been ordained for him.

---

a Some mss read *have turned*.

Preparations for the Flood (5:20–23)

20/ The Lord said that he would obliterate everything on the land—from people to cattle, animals, birds, and whatever moves about on the ground. 21/ He ordered Noah to make himself an ark in order to save himself from the floodwaters. 22/ Noah made an ark in every respect as he had ordered him during the *twenty-seventh*[a] jubilee of years, in the fifth week, during its fifth year [1307]. 23/ He entered (it) during its sixth (year) [1308], in the second month—on the first of the second month until the sixteenth. He and all that we brought to him entered the ark. The Lord closed it from outside on the seventeenth in the evening.

The Flood Itself (5:24–32)

24/ The Lord opened the seven floodgates of heaven and the openings of the sources of the great deep—there being seven openings in number. 25/ The floodgates began to send water down from the sky for 40 days and 40 nights, while the sources of the deep brought waters up until the whole earth was full of water. 26/ The waters increased on the earth; the waters rose 15 cubits above every high mountain. The ark rose above the earth and moved about on the surface of the waters. 27/ The waters remained standing on the surface of the earth for five months—150 days. 28/ Then the ark came to rest on the summit of Lubar, one of the mountains of Ararat. 29/ During the fourth month the sources of the great deep were closed, and the floodgates of heaven were held back. On the first of the seventh month all the sources of the earth's deep places were opened, and the waters started to go down into the deep below. 30/ On the first of the tenth month the summits of the mountains became visible, and on the first of the first month the earth became visible. 31/ The waters dried up from above the earth in the fifth week, in its seventh year [1309]. On the seventeenth day of the second

---

a The Eth mss have a strange reading: *in the second jubilee—years*. Jubilees 6:18 indicates that the jubilee period in question must be the twenty-seventh.

month the earth was dry. 32/ On its twenty-seventh (day) he opened the ark and sent from it the animals, birds, and whatever moves about.

Covenant, the Festival of Weeks, and the 364-Day Calendar (Chapter 6)

Noah's Sacrifice and the Covenant (6:1–4)

6:1/ On the first of the third month he left the ark and built an altar on this mountain. 2/ He made atonement[a] for the earth, took a kid and atoned with its blood for all the sins of the earth because everything that was on it had been obliterated except those who were in the ark with Noah. 3/ He placed the fat on the altar. Then he took a bull, a ram, a sheep, goats, salt, a turtledove, and a dove and offered (them as) a burnt offering on the altar. He was pouring on them an offering mixed with oil, sprinkled wine, and put frankincense on everything. He sent up a pleasant fragrance that was pleasing before the Lord. 4/ The Lord smelled the pleasant fragrance and made a covenant with him that there would be no floodwaters that would destroy the earth; (that) throughout all the days of the earth seedtime and harvest would not cease; (that) cold and heat, summer and winter, day and night would not change their prescribed pattern and would never cease.

Conditions of the Covenant and Confirmation of It by Oath (6:5–10)

5/ "Now you increase and multiply yourselves on the earth and become numerous upon it. Become a blessing within (it). I will put fear of you and dread of you on everything that is on the earth and in the sea. 6/ I have now given you all the animals, all the cattle, everything that flies, everything

---

a Most of the Eth mss have *He appeared* [*'astar'aya*]. 1QapGen x:13 reads *he made atonement*. *He made atonement* would be *'astasraya* in Eth. The two verbs are similar in appearance and were confused in the history of transmitting the text.

that moves about on the earth, the fish in the waters, and everything for food. Like the green herbs I have given you everything to eat. 7/ But you are not to eat animate beings with their spirit—with the blood—because the vital force of all animate beings is in the blood so that your blood with your vital forces may not be required from the hand of any human being. From the hand of each one I will require the blood of a human being. 8/ The person who sheds the blood of a human being will have his blood shed by a human being because he made humanity in the image of God. 9/ As for you—increase and become numerous on the earth."

10/ Noah and his sons swore an oath not to consume any blood that was in any animate being. During this month he made a covenant before the Lord God forever throughout all the history of the earth.

Moses, Israel, the Covenant, and Blood (6:11–14)

11/ For this reason he told you, too, to make a covenant—accompanied by an oath—with the Israelites during this month on the mountain and to sprinkle blood on them because of all the words of the covenant that the Lord was making with them for all times. 12/ This testimony has been written regarding you to keep it for all times so that you may not at any time eat any blood of animals or birds throughout all the days of the earth. (As for) the human being who has eaten the blood of an animal, of cattle, or of birds during all the days of the earth—he and his descendants will be uprooted from the earth.

13/ Now you command the Israelites not to eat any blood so that their name and their descendants may continue to exist before the Lord our God for all time. 14/ This law has no temporal limits because it is forever. They are to keep it throughout history so that they may continue supplicating for themselves with blood in front of the altar each and every day. In the morning and in the evening they are continually to ask pardon for themselves before the Lord so that they may keep it and not be uprooted.

The Sign of the Covenant and the Festival of Weeks (6:15–22)

15/ He gave Noah and his sons a sign that there would not again be a flood on the earth. 16/ He put his bow in the clouds as a sign of the eternal covenant that there would not henceforth[a] be floodwaters on the earth for the purpose of destroying it throughout all the days of the earth. 17/ For this reason it has been ordained and written on the heavenly tablets that they should celebrate the Festival of Weeks during this month—once a year—to renew the covenant each and every year. 18/ This entire festival had been celebrated in heaven from the time of creation until the lifetime of Noah—for 26 jubilees and five weeks of years [= 1309]. Then Noah and his sons kept it for seven jubilees and one week of years until Noah's death [= 350 years]. From the day of Noah's death his sons corrupted (it) until Abraham's lifetime and were eating blood. 19/ Abraham alone kept (it), and his sons Isaac and Jacob kept it until your lifetime. During your lifetime the Israelites forgot (it) until I renewed (it) for them at this mountain.

20/ Now you command the Israelites to keep this festival during all their generations as a commandment for them: one day in the year, during this month, they are to celebrate the festival, 21/ because it is the Festival of Weeks and it is the Festival of Firstfruits. This festival is twofold and of two kinds. Celebrate it as it is written and inscribed regarding it. 22/ For I have written (this) in the book of the first law in which I wrote for you that you should celebrate it at each of its times one day in a year. I have told you about its sacrifice so that the Israelites may continue to remember and celebrate it throughout their generations during this month—one day each year.

The Four Memorial Days and Days of Seasons (6:23–31)

23/ On the first of the first month, the first of the fourth month, the first of the seventh month, and the first of the tenth

---

a Or *therefore*. Some Eth mss omit the word.

month are memorial days and days of the seasons. They are written down and ordained at the four divisions of the year as an eternal testimony. 24/ Noah ordained them as festivals for himself throughout the history of eternity with the result that through them he had a reminder. 25/ On the first of the first month he was told to make the ark, and on it the earth became dry, he opened (it), and saw the earth. 26/ On the first of the fourth month the openings of the depths of the abyss below were closed. On the first of the seventh month all the openings of the earth's depths[a] were opened, and the water began to go down into them. 27/ On the first of the tenth month the summits of the mountains became visible, and Noah was very happy.

28/ For this reason he ordained them for himself forever as memorial festivals. So they are ordained, 29/ and they enter them on the heavenly tablets. Each one of them (consists of) 13 weeks; their memorial (extends) from one to the other: from the first to the second, from the second to third, and from the third to the fourth. 30/ All the days of the commandments will be 52 weeks of days; (they will make) the entire year complete. 31/ So it has been engraved and ordained on the heavenly tablets. One is not allowed to transgress a single year, year by year.

The 364-Day Calendar and Warnings about Deviations from It (6:32-38)

32/ Now you command the Israelites to keep the years in this number—364 days. Then the year will be complete and it will not disturb its time from its days or from its festivals because everything will happen in harmony with their testimony. They will neither omit a day nor disturb a festival. 33/ If they transgress and do not celebrate them in accord with his command, then all of them will disturb their times. The years will be moved from this; they will disturb the

---

a The words *On the first of the seventh month all the openings of the earth's depths* are omitted by many excellent mss.

times and the years will be moved. They will transgress their prescribed pattern. 34/ All the Israelites will forget and will not find the way of the years. They will forget the first of the month, the season, and the Sabbath; they will err with respect to the entire prescribed pattern of the years. 35/ For I know and from now on will inform you—not from my own mind because this is the way the book is written in front of me, and the divisions of times are ordained on the heavenly tablets, lest they forget the covenantal festivals and walk in the festivals of the nations, after their error and after their ignorance. 36/ There will be people who carefully observe the moon with lunar observations because it is corrupt (with respect to) the seasons and is early from year to year by ten days. 37/ Therefore years will come about for them when they will disturb (the year) and make a day of testimony something worthless and a profane day a festival. Everyone will join together both holy days with the profane and the profane day with the holy day, for they will err regarding the months, the Sabbaths, the festivals, and the jubilee.

38/ For this reason I am commanding you and testifying to you so that you may testify to them because after your death your children will disturb (it) so that they do not make the year (consist of) 364 (days) only. Therefore, they will err regarding the first of the month, the season, the Sabbath, and the festivals. They will eat all the blood with all (kinds of) meat.

Noah and His Family after the Flood (Chapter 7)

Celebration with Sacrifice and Wine (7:1–6)

7:1/ During the seventh week, in its first year, in this jubilee [1317] Noah planted a vineyard at the mountain whose name was Lubar, one of the mountains of Ararat, on which the ark had come to rest. It produced fruit in the fourth year [1320]. He guarded its fruit and picked it that year during the seventh month. 2/ He made wine from it, put it in a container, and kept it until the fifth year [1321]—until the first day at the beginning of the first month. 3/ He joyfully celebrated the day of this festival. He made a burnt offering for the

Lord—one young bull, one ram, seven sheep each a year old, and one kid—to make atonement through it for himself and for his sons. 4/ First he prepared the kid. He put some of its blood on the *horns*[a] (that were on) the altar that he had made. He offered all the fat on the altar where he made the burnt offering along with the bull, the ram, and the sheep. He offered all their meat on the altar. 5/ On it he placed their entire sacrifice mixed with oil. Afterwards he sprinkled wine in the fire that had been on the altar beforehand. He put frankincense on the altar and offered a pleasant fragrance that was pleasing before the Lord his God. 6/ He was very happy, and he and his sons happily drank some of this wine.

Noah's Drunkenness and Its Results for His Sons (7:7–17)

7/ When evening came, he went into his tent. He lay down drunk and fell asleep. He was uncovered in his tent as he slept. 8/ Ham saw his father Noah naked and went out and told his two brothers outside. 9/ Then Shem took some clothes, rose—he and Japheth—and they put the clothes on their shoulders as they were facing backwards. They covered their father's shame as they were facing backwards.

10/ When Noah awakened from his sleep, he realized everything that his youngest son had done to him. He cursed his son and said: "Cursed be Canaan. May he become an abject slave to his brothers." 11/ Then he blessed Shem and said: "May the Lord, the God of Shem, be blessed. May Canaan become his slave. 12/ May the Lord enlarge Japheth, and may the Lord live in the place where Shem resides. May Canaan become their slave." 13/ When Ham realized that his father had cursed his youngest son, it was displeasing to him that he had cursed his son. He separated from his father—he and with him his sons Cush, Mizraim, Put, and Canaan. 14/ He built himself a city and named it after his wife Neelatamauk.

---

a At *on the horns* the mss read *on the flesh*. The mistaken reading arose when two Greek words were confused: *krea* (*flesh, meat*; pl. *kreata*) and *kerata* (*horns*). See William K. Gilders, "Where Did Noah Place the Blood? A Textual Note on *Jubilees* 7:4," *JBL* 124 (2005) 745–49.

15/ When Japheth saw (this), he was jealous of his brother. He, too, built himself a city and named it after his wife Adataneses. 16/ But Shem remained with his father Noah. He built a city next to his father at the mountain. He, too, named it after his wife Sedeqatelebab. 17/ Now these three cities were near Mount Lubar: Sedeqatelebab in front of the mountain on its east side; Naeletamauk toward its south side; and Adataneses towards the west.

The Sons of Shem and Japheth (7:18–19)

18/ These were Shem's sons: Elam, Asshur, Arpachshad (he *was born*[a] two years after the flood), Aram, and Lud. 19/ Japheth's sons were: Gomer, Magog, Madai, *Javan, Tubal*,[b] Meshech, and Tiras. These were Noah's sons.

Noah's Address to His Sons and Grandsons (7:20–39)

20/ During the twenty-eighth jubilee [1324–72] Noah began to prescribe for his grandsons the ordinances and the commandments—every statute that he knew. He testified to his sons that they should do what is right, cover the shame of their bodies, bless the one who had created them, honor father and mother, love one another, and keep themselves from fornication, impurity, and from all injustice. 21/ For it was on account of these three things that the flood was on the earth, since (it was) due to fornication that the Watchers had illicit intercourse—apart from the mandate of their authority—with women. When they married of them whomever they chose they committed the first (acts) of impurity. 22/ They fathered (as their) sons the Nephilim. All of them were dissimilar (from one another) and would devour one another: the giant killed the Naphil; the Naphil killed the Elyo; the Elyo humanity; and people their fellows. 23/ When everyone sold himself to commit injustice and to shed innocent blood,

---

a The mss read *tewledd* (*generation*), whereas *tawalda* (*was born*) is needed.

b The mss represent the two names as one word, whereas the two are distinguished in Jub 9:10–11.

the earth was filled with injustice. 24/ After them all the animals, birds, and whatever moves about and whatever walks on the earth. Much blood was shed on the earth. All the thoughts and wishes of humanity were (devoted to) thinking up what was useless and wicked all the time. 25/ Then the Lord obliterated all from the surface of the earth because of their actions and because of the blood that they had shed in the earth.

26/ "We—I and you, my children, and all who entered the ark with us—were left. But now I am the first to see your actions—that you have not been conducting yourselves properly because you have begun to conduct yourselves in the way of destruction, to separate from one another, to be jealous of one another, and not to be together with one another, my sons. 27/ For I myself see that the demons have begun to lead you and your children astray; and now I fear regarding you that after I have died you will shed human blood on the earth and (that) you yourselves will be obliterated from the surface of the earth. 28/ For everyone who sheds human blood and everyone who consumes the blood of any animate being will all be obliterated from the earth. 29/ No one who consumes blood or who sheds blood on the earth will be left. He will be left with neither descendants nor posterity living beneath heaven because they will go into Sheol and will descend into the place of judgment. All of them will depart into deep darkness through an evil death. 30/ No blood of all the blood that there may be at any time when you sacrifice any animal, cattle, or (creature) that flies above the earth is to be seen on you. Do a good deed for yourselves by covering what is poured out on the surface of the earth. 31/ Do not be one who eats (meat) with the blood; exert yourselves so that blood is not consumed in your presence. Cover the blood because so was I ordered to testify to you and your children together with all humanity. 32/ Do not eat the life with the meat so that your blood, your life, may not be required from everyone who sheds (blood) on the earth. 33/ For the earth will not be purified of the blood which has been shed on it; but by the blood of the one who shed it the earth will be purified in all its generations.

34/ "Now listen, my children. Do what is just and right so that you may be rightly planted on the surface of the entire earth. Then your honor will be raised before my God who saved me from the floodwaters. 35/ You will now go and build yourselves cities, and in them you will plant every (kind of) plant that is on the earth as well as every (kind of) fruit tree. 36/ For three years its fruit will remain unpicked by anyone for the purpose of eating it; but in the fourth year its fruit will be sanctified. It will be offered as firstfruits that are acceptable before the Most High God, the Creator of heaven, the earth, and everything, so that they may offer in abundance the first of the wine and oil as firstfruits on the altar of the Lord who accepts (it). What is left over those who serve in the Lord's house are to eat before the altar that receives (it). 37/ During the fifth year arrange relief for it so that you may leave it in the right and proper way. Then you will be doing the right thing, and all your planting will be successful. 38/ For this is how Enoch, the ancestor of your father, commanded his son Methuselah; then Methuselah his son Lamech; and Lamech commanded me everything that his fathers had commanded him. 39/ Now I am commanding you, my children, as Enoch commanded his son in the first jubilees, while he was living in its seventh generation." He[a] commanded and testified to his children and grandchildren until the day of his death.

Genealogy and Division of the Earth among Noah's Three Sons (Chapter 8)

Genealogy from Arpachshad to Peleg (8:1–8)

8:1/ In the twenty-ninth jubilee, in the first week—at its beginning [1373]—Arpachshad married a woman named Rasueya, the daughter of Susan, the daughter of Elam. She gave birth to

---

a By ending Noah's direct speech with the sentence before this final one in v 39, a problematic implication of the text is avoided: it sounds as if Enoch is the referent of *He*, and the line claims that he died. In Gen 5:24 and Jub 4:23–24 Enoch does not die but is removed. If *He* refers to Noah, there is no problem, since he died.

JUBILEES 8:1–9

a son for him in the third year of this week [1375], and he named him Kainan. 2/ When the boy grew up, his father taught him (the art of) writing. He went to look for a place of his own where he could possess his own city. 3/ He found an inscription that the ancients had incised in a rock. He read what was in it, copied it, and sinned on the basis of what was in it, since in it was the Watchers' teaching by which they used to observe the omens of the sun, moon, and stars and every heavenly sign. 4/ He wrote (it) down[a] but told it to no one because he was afraid to tell Noah about it lest he become angry at him for it.

5/ In the thirtieth jubilee, in the second week—in its first year [1429]—he married a woman whose name was Melcha, the daughter of Madai, Japheth's son. In its fourth year [1432] he became the father of a son whom he named Shelah, for he said: "I have truly been sent." 6/ After he was born in the fourth year, Shelah grew up and married a woman whose name was Muak, the daughter of Kesed, his father's brother, in the *thirty-first*[b] jubilee, in the fifth week, in its first year [1499]. 7/ She gave birth to a son for him in its fifth year [1503], and he named him Eber. He married a woman whose name was Azura, the daughter of Nebrod, during the thirty-second jubilee, in the seventh week, during its third year [1564].

8/ In the sixth year [1567] she gave birth to a son for him, and he named him Peleg because at the time when he was born Noah's children began to divide the earth for themselves. For this reason he named him Peleg.

Division of the Earth among Noah's Sons (8:9–30)

Improper Division (8:9)

9/ They divided it in a bad way among themselves and told Noah.

---

a Some excellent mss read *they wrote (it) down*, apparently referring to the Watchers.

b Most mss offer the reading *in the year and in the thirtieth*. The context shows, however, that the jubilee in question is the thirty-first.

Proper Division (8:10–30)

Introduction (8:10–11)

10/ At the beginning of the thirty-third jubilee [1569–1617] they divided the earth into three parts—for Shem, Ham, and Japheth—each in his own inheritance. (This happened) in the first year of the first week [1569] while one of us who were sent was staying with them.

11/ When he summoned his children, they came to him—they and their children. He divided the earth into the lots that his three sons would occupy. They reached out their hands and took the book from the bosom of their father Noah.

Shem's Lot (8:12–21)

12/ In the book there emerged as Shem's lot the center of the earth that he would occupy as an inheritance for him and for his children throughout the history of eternity: from the middle of the mountain range of Rafa, from the source of the water from the Tina River. His share goes toward the west through the middle of this river. One then goes until one reaches the water of the deeps from which this river emerges. This river emerges and pours its waters into the Me'at Sea. This river goes as far as the Great Sea. Everything to the north belongs to Japheth, while everything to the south belongs to Shem. 13/ It goes until it reaches Karas. This is in the bosom of the branch that faces southward. 14/ His share goes toward the Great Sea and goes straight until it reaches to the west of the branch that faces southward, for this is the sea whose name is the Branch of the Egyptian Sea. 15/ It turns from there southwards toward the mouth of the Great Sea on the shore of the waters. It goes toward the west of Afra and goes until it reaches the water of the Gihon River and to the south of the Gihon's waters along the banks of this river. 16/ It goes eastward until it reaches the Garden of Eden, toward the south side of it—on the south and from the east of the entire land of Eden and of all the east. It turns to the east and comes until it reaches to the east of the mountain range named Rafa. Then it goes down toward the bank of the Tina River's mouth.

17/ This share emerged by lot for Shem and his children to occupy it forever, throughout history until eternity. 18/ Noah was very happy that this share had emerged for Shem and his children. He recalled everything that he had said in prophecy with his mouth, for he had said: "May the Lord, the God of Shem, be blessed, and may the Lord live in the places where Shem resides." 19/ He knew that the Garden of Eden is the holy of holies and is the residence of the Lord; (that) Mount Sinai is in the middle of the desert; and (that) Mount Zion is in the middle of the navel of the earth. The three of them— the one facing the other—were created as holy (places). 20/ He blessed the God of gods, who had placed the word of the Lord in his mouth and (he blessed) the Lord forever. 21/ He knew that a blessed and excellent share had fallen to the lot of Shem and his children throughout the history of eternity: all the land of Eden, all the land of the Erythrean Sea, all the land of the east, India, (that which is) in Erythrea and its mountains, all the land of Bashan, all the land of Lebanon, the islands of Caphtor, the entire mountain range of Sanir and Amana, the mountain range of Asshur that is in the north, all the land of Elam, Asshur, Babylon, Susan, and Madai; all the mountains of Ararat, all the area on the other side of the sea that is on the other side of the mountain range of Asshur toward the north—a blessed and spacious land. Everything in it is very beautiful.

Ham's Lot (8:22–24)

22/ For Ham there emerged a second share toward the other side of the Gihon—toward the south—on the right side of the garden. It goes southward and goes to all the fiery mountains. It goes westward toward the Atel Sea; it goes westward until it reaches the Mauk Sea, everything that descends into which *is*[a] destroyed. 23/ It comes to the north to the boundary of Gadir and comes to the shore of the sea waters, to the waters of the Great Sea, until it reaches the Gihon River. The

---

a The text reads *is not*, although some mss omit *not*. A Syr citation of the verse has *is*, which suits the context.

Gihon River goes until it reaches the right side of the Garden of Eden.

24/ This is the land that emerged for Ham as a share that he would occupy for himself and his children forever throughout their generations until eternity.

Japheth's Lot (8:25–29)

25/ For Japheth there emerged a third share on the other side of the Tina River toward the north of the mouth of its waters. It goes toward the northeast, (toward) the whole area of Gog and all that is east of them. 26/ It goes due north and goes toward the mountains of Qelt, to the north and toward the Mauq Sea. It comes to the east of Gadir as far as the edge of the sea waters. 27/ It goes until it reaches the west of Fara. Then it goes back toward Aferag and goes eastward toward the water of the Me'at Sea. 28/ It goes to the edge of the Tina River toward the northeast until it reaches the bank of its waters toward the mountain range of Rafa. It goes around the north.

29/ This is the land that emerged for Japheth and his children as his hereditary share which he would occupy for himself and his children throughout their generations forever: five large islands and a large land in the north.

Summary (8:30)

30/ However, it is cold while the land of Ham is hot. Now Shem's land is neither hot nor cold but it is a mixture of cold and heat.

Division of the Brothers' Shares among Their Sons (Chapter 9)

Ham Divides His Share among His Four Sons (9:1)

9:1/ Ham divided (his share) among his sons. There emerged a first share for Cush to the east; to the west of him (one) for Egypt;

to the west of him (one) for Put; to the west of him (one) for Canaan; and to the west of him was the sea.

Shem Divides His Share among His Five Sons (9:2–6)

2/ Shem, too, divided (his share) among his sons. There emerged a first share for Elam and his children to the east of the Tigris River until it reaches the east, the entire land of India, in Erythrea on its border, the waters of Dedan, all the mountains of Mebri and Ela, all the land of Susan, and everything on the border of Farnak as far as the Erythrean Sea and the Tina River. 3/ For Asshur there emerged as the second share the whole land of Asshur, Nineveh, Shinar, and Sak[a] as far as the vicinity of India, (where) the Wadafa River[b] rises. 4/ For Arpachshad there emerged as a third share all the land of the Chaldean region to the east of the Euphrates that is close to the Erythrean Sea; all the waters of the desert as far as the vicinity of the branch of the sea that faces Egypt; the entire land of Lebanon, Sanir, and Amana as far as the vicinity of the Euphrates. 5/ There emerged for Aram as the fourth share the entire land of Mesopotamia between the Tigris and Euphrates to the north of the Chaldeans as far as the vicinity of the mountain range of Asshur and the land of Arara. 6/ For Lud there emerged as the fifth share the mountain range of Asshur and all that belongs to it until it reaches the Great Sea and reaches to the east of his brother Asshur.

Japheth Divides His Share among His Seven Sons (9:7–13)

7/ Japheth, too, divided the land among his sons as an inheritance. 8/ There emerged for Gomer a first share eastward from the north side as far as the Tina River. North of him there emerged (as a share) for Magog all the central parts of

---

[a] For a discussion of the reading and the name, see VanderKam, *Book of Jubilees*, 2:56; *Jubilees 1–21*, 386.

[b] For the reading and the name, see the sources listed in the preceding note.

the north until it reaches the Me'at Sea. 9/ For Madai there emerged a share for him to occupy on the west of his two brothers as far as the islands and the shores of the islands. 10/ For Javan there emerged as the fourth share every island and the islands that are in the direction of Lud's border. 11/ For Tubal there emerged as the fifth share the middle of the branch that reaches the border of Lud's share as far as the second branch, and the other side of the second branch into the third branch. 12/ For Meshech there emerged a sixth share, namely, all the (region on the) other side of the third branch until it reaches to the east of Gadir. 13/ For Tiras there emerged as the seventh share the four large islands within the sea that reach Ham's share. The islands of Kamaturi emerged by lot for Arpachshad's children as his inheritance.

Noah Makes His Sons and Grandsons Swear an Oath Cursing Violators of the Boundaries Assigned (9:14–15)

14/ In this way Noah's sons divided (the earth) for their sons in front of their father Noah. He made (them) swear by oath to curse each and every one who wanted to occupy the share that did not emerge by his lot. 15/ All of them said: "So be it. So be it for them and their children until eternity during their generations until the day of judgment on which the Lord God will punish them with the sword and fire because of all the evil impurity of their errors by which they have filled the earth with wickedness, impurity, fornication, and sin."

The Demons, the Tower of Babel, and Occupying the Earth (Chapter 10)

Noah's Descendants, the Demons, and Mastema (10:1–14)

10:1/ During the third week of this jubilee [1583–89] impure demons began to mislead Noah's grandchildren, to make them act foolishly, and to destroy them. 2/ Then Noah's sons came to their father Noah and told him about the demons who were misleading, blinding, and killing his grandchildren. 3/ He prayed before the Lord his God and said, "God of the spirits which are in all animate beings—you who have shown kindness to me, saved me and my sons from the floodwaters, and did not make me perish as you did to the people (meant for) destruction—because your mercy for me has been large and your kindness to me has been great: may your mercy be lifted over the children of your children; and may the wicked spirits not rule them in order to destroy them from the earth. 4/ Now you bless me and my children so that we may increase, become numerous, and fill the earth. 5/ You know how your Watchers, the fathers of these spirits, have acted during my lifetime. As for these spirits who have remained alive, shut them up and hold them captive in the place of judgment. May they not cause destruction among your servant's sons, my God, for they are depraved and were created for the purpose of destroying. 6/ May they not rule the spirits of the living for you alone know their punishment; and may they not have power over the sons of the righteous from now and forevermore." 7/ Then our God told us to imprison each one.

8/ When Mastema, the leader of the spirits, came, he said, "Lord Creator, leave some of them before me; let them listen to me and do everything that I tell them, because if none of them is left for me I shall not be able to exercise the authority of my will among humanity. For they are meant for (the purposes of) destroying and misleading before my punishment because the evil of humanity is great." 9/ Then he said that a tenth of them should be left before him, while he would make nine parts descend to the place of judgment. 10/ He told one of us that we should teach Noah all their medicines because he knew that they would neither conduct themselves properly nor contend fairly. 11/ We acted in accord with his entire command. All of the evil ones who were depraved we imprisoned in the place of judgment, while we left a tenth of them to exercise power on the earth before the satan. 12/ We told Noah all the medicines for their diseases with their deceptions so that he could cure (them) by means of the earth's plants. 13/ Noah wrote down in a book everything (just) as we had taught him regarding all the kinds of medicine, and the evil spirits were stopped from pursuing Noah's children. 14/ He gave all the books that he had written to his oldest son Shem because he loved him much more than all his sons.

The Death of Noah (10:15–17)

15/ Noah slept with his fathers and was buried on Mount Lubar in the land of Ararat. 16/ He completed 950 years in his lifetime—19 jubilees, two weeks, and five years—17/ (he) who lived longer on the earth than (other) people except Enoch because of his righteousness in which he was perfect (i.e.,) in his righteousness; because Enoch's work was something created as a testimony for the generations of eternity so that he should report all deeds throughout generation after generation on the day of judgment.

The Tower of Babel (10:18–26)

18/ During the thirty-third jubilee, in the first year in this second week [1576], Peleg married a woman whose name was Lomna, the daughter of Sinaor. She gave birth to a son for him in the fourth year of this week [1579], and he named him Ragew, for he said, "Humanity has now become evil through the perverse plan to build themselves a city and tower in the land of Shinar." 19/ For they had emigrated from the land of Ararat toward the east, to Shinar, because in his lifetime they built the city and the tower, saying, "Let us ascend through it to heaven." 20/ They began to build. In the fourth week [1590–96] they used fire for baking and bricks served them as stones. The mud with which they were plastering was asphalt that comes from the sea and from the water springs in the land of Shinar. 21/[a] They continued building for 43 years.

---

a Because of several mistakes in the Ethiopic tradition of the text, the verse makes little sense in the readings of the mss. A Greek citation of the passage provides a clearer

The height was 5,433 cubits and two spans, the width about 203 bricks; the height of the brick was a third of one brick; the extent of one wall was thirteen stades and of the other thirty.

22/ Then the Lord our God said to us, "The people here are one, and they have begun to work. Now nothing will elude them. Come, let us go down and confuse their languages so that they do not understand one another and are dispersed into cities and nations and one plan no longer remains with them until the day of judgment." 23/ So the Lord went down and we went down with him to see the city and the tower that humanity had built. 24/ He confused every sound of their languages; no one any longer understood what the other was saying. Then they stopped building the city and the tower. 25/ For this reason the whole land of Shinar was named Babel because there God confused all the languages of humanity. From there they were dispersed into their cities, each according to their languages and their nations. 26/ The Lord sent a wind[a] at the tower and tipped it to the ground. It is now between Asshur and Babylon, in the land of Shinar. He named it Collapse.

Canaan Steals Land from Arpachshad (10:27–34)

27/ In the fourth week, during the first year—at its beginning—of the thirty-fourth jubilee [1639], they were dispersed from the land of Shinar. 28/ Ham and his sons went into the land that he was to occupy, which he had acquired as his share, in the southern country. 29/ When Canaan saw that the land of Lebanon as far as the stream of Egypt was very beautiful, he did not go to his hereditary land to the west of the sea. He settled in the land of Lebanon, on the east and west, from

---

text. The translation is based on this citation in the Catena to Genesis, comment on Gen 11:4 (Petit, *La chaîne*, 2:202, #839). There is a full discussion of the readings in *Jubilees 1–21*, 414.

a Some mss call it *a great wind*.

the border of the Jordan and on the seacoast. 30/ His father Ham and his brothers Cush and Mizraim said to him, "You have settled in a land that was not yours and did not emerge for us by lot. Do not act this way, for if you do act this way both you and your children will fall in the land and be cursed with dissension, because you have settled in dissension and in dissension your children will fall and be uprooted forever. 31/ Do not settle in Shem's residence because it emerged by their lot for Shem and his sons. 32/ You are cursed and will be cursed more than all of Noah's children through the curse by which we obligated ourselves with an oath before the Holy Judge and before your father Noah." 33/ But he did not listen to them. He settled in the land of Lebanon—from Hamath to the entrance of Egypt—he and his sons until the present. 34/ For this reason that land was named the land of Canaan.

Madai Requests and Receives a Different Land (10:35–36)

35/ Japheth and his sons went toward the sea and settled in the land of their share. Madai saw the land near the sea but it did not please him. So he pleaded (for land) from Elam, Asshur, and Arpachshad, his wife's brother. He has settled in the land of Medeqin near his wife's brother until the present. 36/ He named the place where he lived and the place where his children lived Medeqin after their father Madai.

The Shemite Genealogy from Ragew to Abram, the Growth of Evil, and the Early Exploits of Abram (Chapter 11)

The Growth of Wickedness in Serug's Generation (11:1–6)

11:1/ In the thirty-fifth jubilee, during the third week—in its first year [1681]—Ragew married a woman whose name was Ara, the daughter of Ur, Kesed's son. She gave birth to a son for him, and he named him Serug in the seventh *year*[a] of this

---

a The Eth mss read *week*, possibly through confusing and repeating the similar-looking word for *seven*.

week [1687]. 2/ During this jubilee Noah's children began to fight one another, to take captives, and to kill one another; to shed human blood on the earth, to consume blood; to build fortified cities, walls, and towers; men to elevate themselves over peoples, to set up the first kingdoms; to go to war—people against people, nations against nations, city against city; and everyone to do evil, to acquire weapons, and to teach warfare to their sons. City began to capture city and to sell male and female slaves. 3/ Ur,[a] Kesed's son, built the city of Ara of the Chaldeans. He named it after himself and his father. 4/ They made carved images for themselves. Each one would worship the idol that he had made as his own carved image. They began to make statues, images, and unclean things;[b] the spirits of the depraved ones were helping and misleading (them) so that they would commit sins, impurities, and transgression. 5/ Prince Mastema was exerting his power in effecting all these actions and, by means of the spirits, he was sending to those who were placed under his control (the ability) to commit every (kind of) error and sin and every (kind of) transgression; to corrupt, to destroy, and to shed blood on the earth. 6/ For this reason Serug was named Serug: because everyone turned to commit every (kind of) sin.

Genealogy from Serug to Terah (11:7–10)

7/ He grew up and settled in Ur of the Chaldeans near the father of his mother. He was a worshiper of idols. During the thirty-sixth jubilee, in the fifth week, in its first year [1744], he married a woman whose name was Melcha, the daughter of Kaber, the daughter of his father's brother. 8/ She gave birth to Nahor for him during the first year of this week [1744]. He grew up and settled in Ur—in the one that is the Ur of the Chaldeans. His father taught him the studies of the Chaldeans: to practice divination and to augur by the signs

---

    a Almost all of the Eth copies spell the name *Ud*, which resulted when Hebrew *resh* was misread as a *dalet*.

    b Some Eth mss lack the conjunction after *images*, thus reading *images of unclean things*.

of the sky. 9/ During the thirty-seventh jubilee, in the sixth week, in its first year [1800], he married a woman whose name was Iyaseka, the daughter of Nestag of the Chaldeans. 10/ She gave birth to Terah for him in the seventh year of this week [1806].

Mastema's Plague of Ravens (11:11–13)

11/ Then Prince Mastema sent ravens and birds to eat the seed that would be planted in the ground and to destroy the land in order to rob humanity of their labors. Before they plowed in the seed, the ravens would pick (it) from the surface of the ground. 12/ For this reason he named him Terah: because the ravens and birds were reducing them to poverty and eating their seed. 13/ The years began to be unfruitful due to the birds. They would eat all the fruit of the trees from the orchards. During their time, if they were able to save a little of all the fruit of the earth, it was with great effort.

The Birth and Early Days of Abram (11:14–17)

14/ During the thirty-ninth jubilee, in the second week, in the first year [1870], Terah married a woman whose name was Edna, the daughter of Abram, the daughter of his father's sister. 15/ In the seventh year of this week [1876] she gave birth to a son for him, and he named him Abram after his mother's father because he had died before his daughter's son was conceived. 16/ The child began to realize the errors of the earth—that everyone was going astray after the statues and after impurity. His father taught him (the art of) writing. When he was two weeks of years [=14 years], he separated from his father in order not to worship idols with him. 17/ He began to pray to the Creator of all that he would save him from the errors of humanity and that it might not fall to his share to go astray after impurity and wickedness.

Abram and the Ravens (11:18–24)

18/ When the time for planting seeds in the ground arrived, all of them went out together to guard the seed from the ravens.

Abram—a child of 14 years—went out with those who were going out. 19/ As a cloud of ravens came to eat the seed, Abram would run at them before they could settle on the ground. He would shout at them before they could settle on the ground to eat the seed and would say: "Do not come down; return to the place from which you came!" And they returned. 20/ That day he did (this) to the cloud of ravens 70 times. Not a single raven remained in any of the fields where Abram was. 21/ All who were with him in any of the fields would see him shouting; then all of the ravens returned (to their place). His reputation grew large throughout the entire land of the Chaldeans. 22/ All who were planting seed came to him in this year, and he kept going with them until the seedtime came to an end. They planted their land and that year brought in enough food. So they ate and were filled.

23/ In the first year of the fifth week [1891] Abram taught the people who made equipment for bulls—the skillful woodworkers—and they made an implement above the ground, opposite the plow beam, so that one could place seed on it. The seed would then drop down from it onto the end of the plow and be hidden in the ground; and they would no longer be afraid of the ravens. 24/ They made (something) like this above the ground on every plow beam. They planted seed, and all the land did as Abram told them. So they were no longer afraid of the birds.

Abram and the Idols, the Journey to Haran, and the Call to Canaan (Chapter 12)

Abram's Attempt to Convert His Father and Brothers (12:1–8)

12:1/ During the sixth week, in its seventh year [1904], Abram said to his father Terah, "My father." He said, "Yes, my son?" 2/ He said, "What help and advantage do we get from these idols before which you worship and prostrate yourself? 3/ For there is no spirit in them because they are dumb. They are an error of the mind. Do not worship them. 4/ Worship the God of heaven who makes the rain and dew fall on the earth and makes everything on the earth. He created everything by his word; and all life (comes) from his presence. 5/ Why do you worship those things that have no spirit in them? For they are made by hands and you carry them on your shoulders. You receive no help from them, but instead they are a great shame for those who make them and an error of the mind for those who worship them. Do not worship them." 6/ Then he said to him, "I, too, know (this), my son. What shall I do with the people who have ordered me to serve in their presence? 7/ If I tell them what is right, they will kill me because they themselves are attached to them so that they worship and praise them. Be quiet, my son, so that they do not kill you." 8/ When he told these things to his two brothers and they became angry at him, he remained silent.

Marriages of Abram, Haran, and Nahor (12:9–11)

9/ During the fortieth jubilee, in the second week, in its seventh year [1925], Abram married a woman whose name was Sarai, the daughter of his father, and she became his wife. 10/ His brother Haran married a woman in the third year of the third week [1928], and she gave birth to a son for him in the seventh year of this week [1932]. He named him Lot. 11/ His brother Nahor also got married.

Abram Burns the Idol Temple and the Family Leaves Ur (12:12–15)

12/ In the sixtieth[a] year of Abram's life which was the fourth week, in its fourth year [1936], Abram got up at night and burned the temple of the idols. He burned everything in the temple but no one knew (about it). 13/ They got up at night and wanted to save their gods from the fire. 14/ Haran dashed in to save them, but the fire raged over him. He was burned in

---

a The Syr citation of the passage has *56* due to confusion of Syriac letters (Sebastian Brock, "Abraham and the Ravens: A Syriac Counterpart to Jubilees 11–12 and Its Implications," *JSJ* 9 [1978] 148).

the fire and died in *Ur*[a] of the Chaldeans before his father Terah. They buried him in *Ur* of the Chaldeans. 15/ Then Terah left Ur of the Chaldeans—he <u>and</u> his sons—to go to the land of Lebanon and the land of Canaan. He settled in Haran, and Abram lived <u>with</u> his father in Haran for two weeks of years.

Abram Encounters God (12:16–27)

Abram Observes the Stars and Prays to God (12:16–20)

16/ In the sixth week, <u>during</u> its <u>fifth</u> year [1951], Abram sat at night—at the beginning of the seventh month—to observe <u>the stars</u> from evening to dawn in order to see what would be the character of the year with respect to the rains. <u>He</u> was sitting and observing by himself. 17/ A voice came to his mind and he said, "All the signs of <u>the stars</u> and the signs of the moon and the sun—all are under the Lord's control. Why should I be investigating (them)? 18/ If he wishes he will make it rain in the morning and evening; and if he wishes, he will not make it fall. Everything is under his control."

19/ That night he prayed and said:
"My God, my God, God Most High,
You alone are my God.
You have created everything:
Everything that was and has been is the product of your hands.
You and your lordship I have chosen.
20/ Save me from the power of the evil spirits who rule the thoughts of people's minds.
May they not mislead me from following you, my God.
Do establish me and my posterity forever.
May we not go astray from now until eternity."

---

[a] The mss read *'ēnur* (here and later in the verse). The form resulted when in the Greek translation of Jubilees the preposition *en* (*in*) and the name *our* (*Ur*) were combined into one word (Berger, *Jubiläen*, 393 n. d).

Abram Receives the Command to Go to a New Land (12:21–24)

21/ Then he said,[a] "Shall I return to Ur of the Chaldeans who are looking for me to return to them? Or am I to remain here in this place? Make the path that is straight before you prosper through your servant so that he may do (it). May I not proceed in the error of my mind, my God."

22/ When he had finished speaking and praying, then the word of the Lord was sent to him through me: "Now you, come from your land, your family, and your father's house to the land that I will show you. I will make you into a large and numerous people. 23/ I will bless you and magnify your reputation. You will be blessed in the earth. All the nations of the earth will be blessed in you. Those who bless you I will bless, while those who curse you I will curse. 24/ I will be God for you, your son, your grandson, and all your descendants. Do not be afraid. From now until all the generations of the earth I am your God."

Abram Learns Hebrew and Studies His Ancestors' Books (12:25–27)

25/ Then the Lord God said to me, "Open his mouth and his ears to hear and speak with his tongue in the revealed language." For from the day of the Collapse it had disappeared from the mouth(s) of all humanity. 26/ I opened his mouth, ears, and lips and began to speak Hebrew with him—in the language of the creation. 27/ He took his fathers' books—they were written in Hebrew—and copied them. From that time he began to study them, while I was telling him everything that he was unable (to understand). He studied them throughout the six rainy months.

---

a Many Eth copies read *I said*.

Abram and Terah Agree about His Departure for Canaan (12:28–31)

28/ In the seventh year of the sixth week [1953], he spoke with his father and told him that he was leaving Haran to go to the land of Canaan to see it and return to him. 29/ His father Terah said to him:
"Go in peace.
May the eternal God make your way straight;
May the Lord be with you and protect you from every evil;[a]
And may no person have power over you to harm you.
Go in peace."

30/ "If you see a land that, in your view, is a pleasant one in which to live, then come and take me to you. Take Lot, the son of your brother Haran, with you as your son. May the Lord be with you. 31/ Leave your brother Nahor with me until you return in peace. Then all of us together will go with you."

Abram's Travels and Military Adventures (Chapter 13)

Abram's Travels to and in the Land (13:1–9)

13:1/ Abram went from Haran and took his wife Sarai and Lot, the son of his brother Haran, to the land of Canaan. He came to Asur. He walked as far as Shechem and settled near a tall oak tree.[b] 2/ He saw that the land—from the entrance of Hamath to the tall oak—was very pleasant. 3/ Then the Lord said to him, "To you and your descendants I will give this land." 4/ He built an altar there and offered on it a sacrifice to the Lord who had appeared to him.

5/ He departed from there toward the mountain of Bethel that is toward the sea, with Ai toward the east, and pitched his tent there. 6/ He saw that the land was spacious and most

---

a After *from every evil*, the Eth mss contain an additional line for which there is insufficient space on 11Q12 9, lines 5–6: *May he grant you kindness, mercy, and grace before those who see you.*

b The Eth mss offer several unusual words that appear to be combinations of *ḥaba ders* (*near an oak*).

excellent and (that) everything was growing on it: vines, fig trees, pomegranates, oak trees, holm oaks, terebinths, olive trees, cedars, cypresses, incense trees, and all (kinds of) wild trees; and (there was) water on the mountains. 7/ Then he blessed the Lord who had led him from Ur of the Chaldeans and brought him to this mountain.

8/ During the first year in the seventh week [1954]—on the first of the month in which he had initially built the altar on this mountain—he called on the name of the Lord: "You, my God, are the eternal God." 9/ He offered to the Lord a sacrifice on the altar so that he would be with him and not abandon him throughout his entire lifetime.

A Famine and the Journeys to and from Egypt (13:10–16)

10[a]/ He departed from there and went toward the south. When he reached Hebron—Hebron was built at that time—he stayed there for two years. Then he went to the southern territory as far as Baalat. There was a famine in the land. 11/ So Abram went to Egypt in the third year of the week [1956]. He lived in Egypt for five years before his wife was taken from him by force. 12/ Egyptian Tanais was built at that time—seven years after Hebron. 13/ When Pharaoh took Abram's wife Sarai by force for himself, the Lord punished Pharaoh and his household very severely because of Abram's wife Sarai. 14/ Now Abram had an extremely large amount of property: sheep, cattle, donkeys, horses, camels, male and female servants, silver, and very (much) gold. Lot—his brother's son—also had property. 15/ Pharaoh returned Abram's wife Sarai and expelled him from the land of Egypt. He went to the place where he had first pitched his tent—at the location of the altar, with Ai on the east *and* Bethel *on the* west.[b] He blessed the Lord his God who had brought him back safely.

---

a Jubilees 13:10 is where the Lat translation as transcribed by Ceriani begins to be preserved.

b The Lat *a mare* (*on the sea/west*) is the basis for the translation. A number of Eth mss read *and the sea/west*.

16/ During this forty-first jubilee, in the third year of the first week [1963], he returned to this place. He offered a sacrifice on it and called on the Lord's name: "You, Lord, Most High God, are my God forever and ever."

Lot Separates from Abram and Abram Receives Promises (13:17–21)

17/ In the fourth year of this week [1964] Lot separated from him. Lot settled in Sodom. Now the people of Sodom were very sinful. 18/ He was brokenhearted that his brother's son had separated from him for he had no children. 19/ In that year when Lot was taken captive, the Lord spoke to Abram—after Lot had separated from him, in the fourth year of this week—and said to him, "Look up from the place where you have been living toward the north, the south, the west, and the east; 20/ because all the land that you see I will give to you and your descendants forever. I will make your descendants like the sands of the sea. (Even) if a man can count the sands of the earth, your descendants will (still) not be counted. 21/ Get up and walk through its length and its width. Look at everything because I will give it to your descendants." Then Abram went to Hebron and lived there.

War with the Kings and the Tithe (13:22–29)

22/ In this year Chedorlaomer, the king of Elam, Amraphel, the king of Shinar, Arioch, the king of Selasar, and Tergal, the king of the nations came and killed the king of Gomorrah, while the king of Sodom fled. Many people fell with wounds in the *valley* of Saddimaw, in the Salt Sea. 23/ They took captive Sodom, Adamah, and Zeboim; they also took Lot, the son of Abram's brother, captive and all his possessions. He went as far as Dan. 24/ One who had escaped came and told Abram that the son of his brother had been taken captive. 25/ When he had armed his household servants, [Abram went up and killed Chedorlaomer. Upon returning, he took a tithe of everything and gave it to Melchizedek. This tithe was]ᵃ for Abram and his descendants the tithe of the firstfruits for the Lord. The Lord made it an eternal ordinance that they should give it to the priests who serve before him for them to possess it forever. 26/ This law has no temporal limit because he has ordained it for the history of eternity to give a tenth of everything to the Lord—of seed, the vine, oil, cattle, and sheep. 27/ He has given (it) to the priests to eat and to drink joyfully before him.

28/ When the king of Sodom came up to him, he knelt before him and said, "Our lord Abram, kindly give us the people whom you rescued, but their booty is to be yours." 29/ Abram said to him, "I lift my hands to the Most High God (to show that) I will not take anything of yours—not a thread or sandal thongs, so that you may not say, 'I have made Abram rich'—excepting only what the young men have eaten and the share of the men who went with me: Awnan, Eschol, and Mamre. These will take their share."

A Promissory Dream, the Covenant Renewed, and the Birth of Ishmael (Chapter 14)

A Promissory Dream (14:1–6)

14:1/ After these things—in the fourth year of this week [1964], on the first of the third month—the word of the Lord came to Abram in a dream: "Do not be afraid, Abram. I am your protector; your reward will be very large." 2/ He said, "Lord, Lord, what are you going to give me when I go on being childless. The son of Maseq—the son of my maidservantᵇ—that is Damascene Eliezer—will be my heir. You have given me no descendants. Give me descendants." 3/ He said to

---

a It is highly likely that most of the words dealing with the encounter between Abram and Melchizedek have dropped from the text by scribal accident. The text supplied between brackets is based on readings in a few of the Eth copies. For the details, see *Jubilees 1–21*, 467.

b Many Eth mss read *amatiyal* rather than *my maidservant*; possibly it is the name of the woman in question.

him, "This one will not be your heir but rather someone who will come out of your loins will be your heir." 4/ He brought him outside and said to him, "Look at the sky and count the stars if you can count them." 5/ When he had looked at the sky and seen the stars, he said to him, "Your descendants will be like this." 6/ He believed the Lord, and it was credited to him as something righteous.

The Covenant between the Pieces (14:7–20)

7/ He said to him, "I am the Lord who brought you from Ur of the Chaldeans to give you the land of the Canaanites to occupy forever and to be God for you and your descendants after you." 8/ He said, "Lord, Lord, how will I know that I will inherit (it)?" 9/ He said to him, "Get for me a three-year-old calf, a three-year-old goat, a three-year-old sheep, a turtledove, and a dove." 10/ He got all of these in the middle of the month. He was living at the oak of Mamre that is near Hebron. 11/ He built an altar there and sacrificed all of these. He poured their blood on the altar and divided them in the middle. He put them opposite one another, but the birds he did not divide. 12/ Birds kept coming down on what was spread out, but Abram kept preventing them and not allowing the birds to touch them.

13/ At sunset, a terror fell on Abram; indeed a great, dark fear fell on him. It was said to Abram: "Know for a fact that your descendants will be aliens in a foreign land. They will enslave them and oppress them for 400 years. 14/ But I will judge the nation whom they serve. Afterwards, they will leave from there with many possessions. 15/ But you will go peacefully to your fathers and be buried at a ripe old age. 16/ In the fourth generation they will return to this place because until now the sins of the Amorites have not been completed." 17/ When he awakened and got up, the sun had set. There was a flame and an oven was smoking. Fiery flames passed between what was spread out. 18/ On that day the Lord concluded a covenant with Abram with these words: "To your descendants I will give this land from the river of Egypt as far as the great river, the Euphrates River: that of the Kenites, the Kenizzites, the Kadmonites, the Perizzites, the Rephaim, the Phakorites, the Hivites, the Amorites, the Canaanites, the Girgashites, and the Jebusites."

19/ It passed (along), and Abram offered what had been spread out, the birds, their (cereal) offering, and their libation. The fire devoured them. 20/ During this day we concluded a covenant with Abram like the covenant that we concluded during this month with Noah. Abram renewed the festival and the ordinance for himself forever.

Hagar and Ishmael (14:21–24)

21/ Abram was very happy and told all these things to his wife Sarai. He believed that he would have descendants, but she continued not to have a child. 22/ Sarai advised her husband Abram and said to him, "Go in to my Egyptian slave-girl Hagar; perhaps I will build up descendants for you from her." 23/ Abram listened to his wife Sarai's suggestion and said to her, "Do (as you suggest)." So Sarai took her Egyptian slave-girl Hagar, and gave her to her husband Abram to be his wife. 24/ He went in to her, she became pregnant, and gave birth to a son. He named him Ishmael in the fifth year of this week [1965]. That year was the eighty-sixth year in Abram's life.

Covenant, Name Changes, and Circumcision (Chapter 15)

The Date and Abram's Sacrifice (15:1–2)

15:1/ During the fifth year of the fourth week of this jubilee [1986]—in the third month, in the middle of the month—Abram celebrated the Festival of the Firstfruits of the wheat harvest. 2/ He offered as a new sacrifice on the altar the firstfruits of the food for the Lord—a bull, a ram, and a sheep; (he offered them) on the altar as a sacrifice to the Lord together with their (cereal) offerings and their libations. He offered everything on the altar with frankincense.

The Covenant of Circumcision, Name Changes, and Promises (15:3–24)

Covenant with Abram and Changing of His Name to Abraham (15:3–10)

3/ The Lord appeared to him, and the Lord said to Abram: "I am the God of Shaddai. Please me and be perfect. 4/ I will place my covenant between me and you. I will increase you greatly." 5/ Then Abram fell prostrate. The Lord spoke with him and said: 6/ "My pact is now with you. I will make you[a] the father of many nations. 7/ You will no longer be called Abram; your name from now to eternity is to be Abraham because I have designated you the father of many nations. 8/ I will make you very great. I will make you into nations, and kings shall emerge from you. 9/ I will place my covenant between me and you and your descendants after you throughout their generations and as an eternal pact so that I may be God to you and to your descendants after you. 10/ [To you and your descendants after you I will give][b] the land where you have resided as an alien—the land of Canaan that you will rule forever. I will be their God."

The Law of Circumcision (15:11–14)

11/ Then the Lord said to Abraham: "As for you, keep my covenant—you and your descendants after you. Circumcise all your males; circumcise your foreskins. It will be a sign of my eternal pact (which is) between me and you. 12/ You will circumcise a child on the eighth day—every male in your families: the person (who has been born in your) house, the one whom you purchased with money from any foreigners—whom you have acquired who is not from your descendants. 13/ The person who is born in your house must be

---

a Some Eth mss read *You will become* as in Gen 17:4.

b The words between brackets come from Gen 17:8. They were omitted when a scribe's eye jumped from the expression at the end of v 9 to the same words at the end of the restored section (Charles, *Ethiopic Version*, 51 n. 9).

circumcised; and those whom you purchased with money are to be circumcised. My covenant will be in your flesh as an eternal pact. 14/ The male who has not been circumcised—the flesh of whose foreskin has not been circumcised on the eighth day—that person will be uprooted from his people because he has violated my covenant."

Sarai/Sarah, Isaac, and Ishmael (15:15–22)

15/ The Lord said to Abraham, "Your wife Sarai will no longer be called Sarai for her name will be Sarah. 16/ I will bless her. I will give you a son from her and will bless him. He will become a nation, and kings of nations will come from him." 17/ Abraham fell prostrate and was very happy. He said to himself, "Will a son be born to one who is 100 years of age? Will Sarah who is 90 years of age give birth (to a child)?" 18/ (So) Abraham said to the Lord: "I wish that Ishmael could live in your presence." 19/ The Lord said, "Very well, but Sarah, too, will give birth to a son for you and you will name him Isaac. I will establish my covenant with him as an eternal covenant and for his descendants after him. 20/ Regarding Ishmael I have listened to you. I will indeed bless him, increase him, and make him very numerous. He will father 12 princes, and I will make him into a large nation. 21/ But my covenant I will establish with Isaac to whom Sarah will give birth for you at this time next year." 22/ When he had finished speaking with him, the Lord went up from Abraham.

Circumcising the Males of Abraham's Household (15:23–24)

23/ Abraham did as the Lord told him. He took his son Ishmael, everyone who was born in his house and who had been purchased with money—every male who was in his house—and circumcised the flesh of their foreskins. 24/ On the same day Abraham was circumcised; those who were born in his house, the men of his household,[a] and all those who had

---

[a] The Eth mss read just the second of the two expressions containing the word *house*, while Lat, probably correctly (cf. Gen 17:23, 27), has the two rendered here.

been purchased with money even from foreigners were circumcised with him.

The Significance of Circumcision (15:25–34)

25/ This law is (valid) for all history forever. There is no circumcising of days, nor omitting any day of the eight days because it is an eternal ordinance ordained and written on the heavenly tablets. 26/ Anyone who is born the flesh of whose private parts has not been circumcised by the eighth day does not belong to the people of the pact that the Lord made with Abraham but to the people (meant for) destruction. Moreover, there is no sign on him that he belongs to the Lord, but (he is meant) for destruction, for being destroyed from the earth, and for being uprooted from the earth because he has violated the covenant of the Lord our God. 27/ For this is what the nature of all the angels of the presence and all the angels of holiness was like from the day of their creation. In front of the angels of the presence and the angels of holiness he sanctified Israel to be with him and his holy angels.

28/ Now you command the Israelites to keep the sign of this covenant throughout their history as an eternal ordinance so that they may not be uprooted from the earth 29/ because the command has been ordained as a covenant so that they should keep it forever on all the Israelites. 30/ For the Lord did not draw near to himself either Ishmael, his sons, his brothers, or Esau. He did not choose them (simply) because they were among Abraham's children, for he knew them. But he chose Israel to be his people. 31/ He sanctified them and gathered (them) from all humanity. For there are many nations and many peoples and all belong to him. He made spirits rule over all in order to lead them astray from following him. 32/ But over Israel he made no angel or spirit rule because he alone is their ruler. He will guard them and require them for himself from his angels, his spirits, and everyone, and all his powers so that he may guard them and bless them and so that they may be his and he theirs from now and forever.

33/ I am now telling you that the Israelites will prove false to this ordinance. They will not circumcise their sons in accord with this entire law because they will leave some of the flesh of their circumcision when they circumcise their sons. All the people of Belial will leave their sons uncircumcised just as they were born. 34/ Then there will be great anger from the Lord against the Israelites because they abandoned his covenant, departed from his word, provoked, and blasphemed in that they did not perform the ordinance of this sign. For they have made themselves like the nations so as to be removed and uprooted from the earth. They will no longer have forgiveness or pardon so that they should be pardoned and forgiven for every sin, for (their) violation of this eternal (ordinance).

Announcement of Isaac's Birth, Destruction of Sodom, Birth of Isaac, and the Festival of Tabernacles (Chapter 16)

Angelic Announcement regarding the Birth of Isaac (16:1-4)

16:1/ On the first day of the fourth month we appeared to Abraham at the oak of Mamre. We spoke with him and told him that a son would be given to him from his wife Sarah. 2/ Sarah laughed when she heard that we had conveyed this message to Abraham, but when we chided her she became frightened and denied that she had laughed about the message. 3/ We told her the name of her son as it is ordained and written on the heavenly tablets—Isaac— 4/ and (that) when we returned to her at a specific time she would have become pregnant with a son.

Judgment on Sodom, Gomorrah, and Lot's Descendants (16:5-9)

5/ During this month the Lord executed the judgment of Sodom and Gomorrah, Zeboim and all the environs of the Jordan. He burned them with fire and brimstone and annihilated them until the present in accord with what I have now told you (about) all their actions—that they were depraved and very sinful, (that) they would defile themselves, commit sexual sins in their flesh, and do what was impure upon the earth. 6/ The Lord will execute judgment in the same way in the places where people commit the same sort of impure actions as Sodom—just like the judgment on Sodom.[a] 7/ But we went about rescuing Lot because the Lord remembered Abraham. So he brought him out from the overthrow (of Sodom). 8/ He and his daughters committed a sin on the earth that had not occurred on the earth from the time of Adam until his time because the man had sex with his daughter. 9/ Here it has been commanded and engraved on the heavenly tablets regarding all his descendants that he is to remove them, uproot them, execute judgment on them like the judgment of Sodom, and not to leave him any human descendants on the earth on the day of judgment.

Travels, Sarah's Pregnancy, Birth and Circumcision of Isaac (16:10–14)

10/ During this month Abraham migrated from Hebron. He went and settled between Kadesh and Sur in the boundaries[b] of Gerar. 11/ In the middle of the fifth month he migrated from there and settled at the well of the oath. 12/ In the middle of the sixth month the Lord visited Sarah and did for her as he had said. 13/ She became pregnant and gave birth to a son in the third month; in the middle of the month, on the day that the Lord had told Abraham—on the Festival of the Firstfruits of the harvest—Isaac was born. 14/ Abraham circumcised him the eighth day. He was the first to be circumcised according to the covenant that was ordained forever.

Prediction about Abraham's Descendants and a Special Son of Isaac (16:15–19)

15/ In the sixth year of the fourth week [1987] we came to Abraham at the well of the oath. We appeared to him just as we had said to Sarah that we would return to her and she would

---

a At *just like the judgment of Sodom*, Lat reads *he will judge them*.

b This is a place where the Lat and Eth versions reflect a Greek word, *oros*, that, depending on the breathing mark read with it, can mean either *boundary* (so Lat) or *mountain* (so Eth).

have become pregnant with a son. 16/ We had returned during the seventh month, and in front of us we had found Sarah pregnant. We blessed *him* and told *him*[a] everything that had been commanded for him: that he would not yet die until he became the father of six sons and (that) he would see them before he died; but (that) through Isaac he would have a reputation and descendants. 17/ All the descendants of his sons would become nations and be numbered with the nations. But one of Isaac's sons would become a holy progeny and would not be numbered among the nations, 18/ for he would become the share of the Most High. All his descendants had fallen into the (share) that God owns so that they would become a *treasured*[b] people of the Lord out of all the nations; and that they would become a kingdom, a priesthood, and a holy people. 19/ Then we went on our way and told Sarah all that we had reported to him. The two of them were extremely happy.

The Festival of Tabernacles (16:20–31)

20/ There he built an altar for the Lord who had rescued him and who was making him so happy in the country where he resided as an alien. He celebrated a joyful festival in this month—for seven days—near the altar that he had built at the well of the oath. 21/ He constructed tents for himself and his servants during this festival. He was the first to celebrate the Festival of Tabernacles on the earth. 22/ During these seven days he was making—throughout all the days, each and every day—an offering to the Lord on the altar: two bulls, two rams, seven sheep, one goat for sins in order to atone through it for himself and his descendants. 23/ And as a peace offering: seven rams, seven kids, seven sheep, seven he-goats as well as their (cereal) offerings and their libations

---

a him ... him: Almost all of the Eth copies read *her* ... *her*. For the first pronoun Lat has *him* and for the second the ambiguous form *illi*.

b Lat reads *sanctified* and Eth *adornment*. It is likely that both are corruptions of a word meaning *possession* or the like, a reflection of the expression in Exod 19:5; Deut 7:6, etc. (Charles, *Ethiopic Version*, 58 n. 4, 59 n. 2; VanderKam, *Book of Jubilees* 2:98).

over all their fat—(all of these) he would burn on the altar as a choice offering for a pleasing fragrance. 24/ In the morning and evening he would burn fragrant substances: frankincense, galbanum, stacte, nard, myrrh, spikenard, and costum. All seven of these he would offer beaten, equally mixed, pure. 25/ He celebrated this festival for seven days, being happy with his whole heart and all his being—he and all those who belonged to his household. There was no foreigner with him, nor anyone who was uncircumcised. 26/ He blessed his Creator who had created him in his generation because he had created him for his pleasure, for he knew and ascertained that from him there would come a righteous plant for the history of eternity and (that) from him there would be holy descendants so that they should be like the one who had made everything. 27/ He gave a blessing and was very happy. He named this festival the Festival of the Lord—a joy acceptable to the Most High God. 28/ We blessed him eternally and all his descendants who would follow him throughout all the history of the earth because he had celebrated this festival at its time in accord with the testimony of the heavenly tablets. 29/ For this reason it has been ordained on the heavenly tablets regarding Israel that they should celebrate the Festival of Tabernacles joyfully for seven days during the seventh month which is acceptable in the Lord's presence—a law that is eternal throughout their history in each and every year. 30/ This has no temporal limit because it is ordained forever regarding Israel that they should celebrate it, live in tents, place wreaths on their heads, and take leafy branches and willow branches from the stream. 31/ Abraham took palm *branches*[a] and the fruit of good trees, and each and every day he would go around the altar with the branches—seven times per day. In the morning he would give praise and joyfully offer humble thanks to his God for everything.

---

a Eth mss read *the heart of the palms*, and Lat may have done so as well, with the meaning being something like *the central stalks/branches of the palms*. The expression comes from Lev 23:40, where in MT *branches of palm trees* are mentioned (*Jubilees 1–21*, 530).

The Weaning of Isaac, Dismissal of Hagar and Ishmael, and Questions about Abraham's Faithfulness (Chapter 17)

Weaning of Isaac and Expulsion of Hagar and Ishmael (17:1–14)

Weaning Celebration and Sarah's Command (17:1–7)

17:1/ In the first year of the fifth week, in this jubilee [1989], Isaac was weaned. Abraham gave a large banquet in the third month, on the day when his son Isaac was weaned. 2/ Now Ishmael, the son of Hagar the Egyptian, was in his place in front of his father Abraham. Abraham was very happy and blessed the Lord because he saw his own sons and had not died childless. 3/ He remembered the message that he had told him on the day when Lot had separated from him. He was very happy because the Lord had given him descendants on the earth to possess the land. With his full voice he blessed the Creator of everything.

4/ When Sarah saw Ishmael playing and dancing[a] and Abraham being extremely happy, she became jealous of Ishmael. She said to Abraham, "Banish this maidservant and her son because this maidservant's son will not be an heir with my son Isaac." 5/ For Abraham the command regarding his servant girl and his son—that he should banish them from himself—was distressing, 6/ but the Lord said to Abraham: "It ought not to be distressful for you regarding the child and the maidservant. Listen to everything that Sarah says to you and do (it) because through Isaac you will have a reputation and descendants. 7/ Now with regard to this maidservant's son—I will make him into a large nation because he is one of your descendants."

Expulsion and Fate of Hagar and Ishmael (17:8–14)

8/ So Abraham rose early in the morning, took food and a bottle of water, placed them on the shoulders of Hagar and the

---

a At *and dancing* Lat reads *with Isaac*.

child, and sent her away. 9/ She went and wandered about in the wilderness of Beersheba. When the water in the bottle was gone, the child grew thirsty. He was unable to go on and fell. 10/ His mother took him and, going on, she threw him under *a fir tree*.[a] Then she went and sat opposite him at a distance of a bowshot, for she said, "May I not see the death of my child." When she sat down she cried.

11/ An angel of God—one of the holy ones—said to her, "What are you crying about, Hagar? Get up, take the child, and hold him in your arms, because the Lord has heard you and has seen the child." 12/ She opened her eyes and saw a well of water. So she went, filled her bottle with water, and gave her child a drink. Then she set out and went toward the wilderness of Paran. 13/ When the child grew up, he became an archer and the Lord was with him. His mother took a wife for him from the Egyptian girls. 14/ She gave birth to a son for him, and he named him Nebaioth, for she said, "The Lord was close to me when I called to him."

Mastema's Challenge and the Lord's Knowledge about Abraham (17:15–18)

15/ During the seventh week, in the first year during the first month—on the twelfth of this month—in this jubilee [2003], there were words in heaven regarding Abraham, that he was faithful in everything that he had told him, (that) the Lord loved him, and (that) in every difficulty he was faithful. 16/ Then Prince Mastema[b] came and said before God: "Abraham does indeed love his son Isaac and finds him more pleasing than anyone else. Tell him to offer him as a sacrifice on an altar. Then you will see whether he performs this order and will know whether he is faithful in everything through which you test him." 17/ Now the Lord was aware that

---

a The word *'ël(e)yās* in Eth, perhaps a transcription of the Greek word for *olive tree* (*elaias*), may be a mistake for *elatēs* (*pine* or *fir tree*) (Dillmann, "Jubiläen," 71 n. 95; Charles, *Ethiopic Version*, 62 n. 13).

b Several Eth copies read *the prince of Mastema*.

Abraham was faithful in every difficulty which he had told him. For he had tested him through his land and the famine; he had tested him through the wealth of kings; he had tested him again through his wife when she was taken forcibly, and through circumcision; and he had tested him through Ishmael and his servant girl Hagar when he sent them away. 18/ In everything through which he tested him he was found faithful. He himself did not grow impatient, nor was he slow to act; for he was faithful and one who loved the Lord.

The Binding of Isaac (Chapter 18)

The Command to Sacrifice Isaac and the Journey to the Place of Sacrifice (18:1–5)

18:1/ The Lord said to him, "Abraham, Abraham!" He replied, "Yes?" 2/ He said to him, "Take your son, your dear one whom you love—Isaac—and go to a high land.[a] Offer him on one of the mountains that I will make known to you." 3/ So he got up early in the morning, loaded his donkey, and took with him his two servants as well as his son Isaac. He chopped the wood for the sacrifice and came to the place on the third day. He saw the place from a distance. 4/ When he reached a well of water, he ordered his servants: "Stay here with the donkey while I and the child go on. After we have worshiped we will return to you." 5/ He took the wood for the sacrifice and placed it on his son Isaac's shoulders. He took fire and a knife in his hands. The two of them went together to that place.

Preparations for the Sacrifice (18:6–8)

6/ Isaac said to his father, "Father." He replied, "Yes, my son?" He said to him, "Here are the fire, the knife, and the wood, but where is the sheep for the sacrifice, father?" 7/ He said, "The Lord will provide for himself a sheep for the sacrifice, my son." When he neared the place of the mountain of the

---

a Several excellent mss read *mountain* instead of *land*.

Lord, 8/ he built an altar and placed the wood on the altar. Then he tied up his son Isaac, placed him on the wood that was on the altar, and reached out his hands to take the knife in order to sacrifice his son Isaac.

Sacrifice of Isaac Averted and Mastema Shamed (18:9–13)

9/ Then I stood in front of him and in front of the prince of Mastema.[a] The Lord said, "Tell him not to let his hand go down on the child and not to do anything to him because I have shown that he is one who fears the Lord." 10/ So I called to him from heaven and said to him, "Abraham, Abraham!" He was startled and said, "Yes?" 11/ I said to him, "Do not lay your hands on the child and do not do anything to him because I have now shown that you are one who fears the Lord. You have not refused me your son, your firstborn." 12/ The prince of Mastema was put to shame. Then Abraham looked up and saw a ram caught by its horns.[b] Abraham went and took the ram. He offered it as a sacrifice instead of his son. 13/ Abraham named that place "The Lord Saw" so that it is named "The Lord Saw." It is Mount Zion.

Blessings for Abraham (18:14–16)

14/ The Lord again called to Abraham by his name from heaven, just as we had appeared[c] in order to speak to him in the Lord's name. 15/ He said, "I have sworn by myself, says the Lord: because you have performed this command and have not refused me your firstborn son whom you love, I will indeed bless you and will indeed multiply your descendants like the stars in the sky and like the sands on the seashore. Your descendants will possess the cities of their enemies. 16/ All

---

a Some mss read *Prince Mastema*. The same happens in v 12.

b Many Eth mss have *it was coming with its horns*, whereas Lat reads *it was caught by its horns*. See *Jubilees 1–21*, 574.

c Although Lat and many Eth copies have *we* as the subject of the verb, other Eth mss have *he (appeared to us)*.

the nations of the earth will be blessed through your descendants because of the fact that you have obeyed my command. I have made known to everyone that you are faithful to me in everything that I have told you. Go in peace."

Return and Commemorative Festival (18:17–19)

17/ Then Abraham went to his servants. They set out and went together to Beersheba. Abraham lived at the well of the oath. 18/ He used to celebrate this festival joyfully for seven days during all the years. He named it the Festival of the Lord in accord with the seven days during which he went and returned safely. 19/ This is the way it is ordained and written on the heavenly tablets regarding Israel and his descendants: (they are) to celebrate this festival for seven days with festal happiness.

Sarah's Life Ends and Jacob's Begins (Chapter 19)

Death of Sarah and Abraham's Acquisition of a Burial Plot (19:1–9)

19:1/ During the first year of the first week in the forty-second jubilee [2010] Abraham returned and lived opposite Hebron—that is, Kiriath Arba—for two weeks of years. 2/ In the first year of the third week of this jubilee [2024] the days of Sarah's life were completed and she died in Hebron. 3/ When Abraham went to mourn for her and to bury her, we were testing whether he himself was patient and not annoyed in the words that he spoke. But in this respect, too, he was found to be patient and not disturbed, 4/ because he spoke with the Hittites in a patient spirit so that they would give him a place in which to bury his dead. 5/ The Lord gave him a favorable reception before all who would see him. He mildly pleaded with the Hittites, and they gave him the land of the double cave that was opposite Mamre—that is, Hebron—for a price of 400 silver pieces. 6/ They pleaded with him: "Allow us to give (it) to you for nothing!" Yet he did not take (it) from them for nothing but he gave as the price of the place the full amount of money. He bowed twice to them and afterwards buried his dead in the double cave. 7/ All the time of Sarah's life was 127—that is, two jubilees, four weeks, and one year. This was the time in years of Sarah's life.

8/ This was the tenth test by which Abraham was tried, and he was found to be faithful and patient in spirit. 9/ He said nothing about the promise of the land that the Lord said he would give to him and his descendants after him. He pleaded for a place there to bury his dead because he was found to be faithful and was recorded on the heavenly tablets as a friend of the Lord.

Marriages of Isaac and Abraham (19:10–12)

10/ In its fourth year [2027] he took a wife for his son Isaac. Her name was Rebekah, the daughter of Bethuel, the son of Abraham's brother Nahor, the sister of Laban, the daughter of Bethuel; and Bethuel was the son of Milcah who was the wife of Abraham's brother Nahor.[a] 11/ Abraham married a third wife whose name was Keturah—one of the children of his household servants—when Hagar died prior to Sarah. 12/ She gave birth to six sons for him—Zimran, Jokshan, Medai, Midian, Ishbak, and Shuah—during two weeks of years.

Abraham and Jacob (19:13–29)

Birth and Character of Jacob and Esau (19:13–14)

13/ In the sixth week, during its second year [2046], Rebekah gave birth to two sons for Isaac: Jacob and Esau. Jacob was perfect and upright, while Esau was a harsh, rustic, and hairy man. Jacob would live in tents. 14/ When the boys grew up, Jacob learned (the art of) writing, but Esau did not learn (it) because he was a rustic man and a hunter. He learned (the art of) warfare, and everything that he did was harsh.

---

[a] For the textual issues in this convoluted statement about Rebekah's family connections, see *Jubilees 1–21*, 584, 590–91.

Abraham's Assessment of Jacob (19:15–16a)

15/ Abraham loved Jacob but Isaac loved Esau. 16/ As Abraham observed Esau's behavior, he realized that through Jacob he would have a reputation and descendants.

Abraham Speaks to Rebekah about Jacob (19:16b–25)

He summoned Rebekah and gave her orders about Jacob because he saw that she loved Jacob much more than Esau. 17/ He said to her, "My daughter, take care of my son Jacob because he will occupy my place on the earth and (will prove) a blessing among humanity and the glory of all the descendants of Shem. 18/ For I know that the Lord will choose him as his own people (who will be) more enduring[a] than all who are on the surface of the earth. 19/ My son Isaac now loves Esau more than Jacob, but I see that you rightly love Jacob. 20/ Increase your favor to him still more: may your eyes look at him lovingly because he will be a blessing for us on the earth from now and throughout all the history of the earth. 21/ May your hands be strong and your mind be happy with your son Jacob because I love him much more than all my sons; for he will be blessed forever and his descendants will fill the entire earth. 22/ If a person is able to count the sands on the earth, in the same way his descendants, too, will be counted. 23/ May all the blessings with which the Lord blessed me and my descendants belong to Jacob and his descendants for all time. 24/ Through his descendants may my name and the name of my ancestors Shem, Noah, Enoch, Malaleel, Enosh, Seth, and Adam be blessed. 25/ May they serve (the purpose of) laying heaven's foundations, making the earth firm, and renewing all the luminaries which are above the firmament."

Abraham Blesses Jacob (19:26–29)

26/ Then he summoned Jacob into the presence of his mother Rebekah, kissed him, blessed him, and said, 27/ "My dear son

---

a Lat reads *holy*. The passage appears to reflect the expression *'am sĕgullāh* in passages such as Deut 7:6.

Jacob whom I myself love, may God bless you from above the firmament. May he give you all the blessings with which he blessed Adam, Enoch, Noah, and Shem. Everything that he said to me and everything that he promised to give me may he attach to you and your descendants until eternity—like the days of heaven above the earth. 28/ May the spirits of Mastema not rule over you and your descendants to remove you from following the Lord who is your God from now and forever. 29/ May the Lord God be your Father and you his firstborn son and people for all time. Go in peace, my son."

Parental Favorites (19:30–31)

30/ The two of them departed together from Abraham. 31/ Rebekah loved Jacob with her entire heart and her entire being very much more than Esau; but Isaac loved Esau much more than Jacob.

Abraham's Testament to All His Sons and Grandsons (Chapter 20)

Abraham Assembles His Sons and Grandsons (20:1)

20:1/ During the forty-second jubilee, in the first year of the seventh week [2052], Abraham summoned Ishmael and his twelve children, Isaac and his two children, and the six children of Keturah and their sons.

A Report about Abraham's Commands to His Sons and Grandsons (20:2–5)

2/ He ordered them to keep the way of the Lord so that they would do what is right and that they should love one another; that they should be like this in every war so that they could go against each one *who rises*[a] against them; and do what is

---

a The emendation *who rises* follows a suggestion of Werman (*Jubilees*, 330 n. 2) that the Heb word so translated (*hā-'ōleh*) dropped from the text because it looks much like the next word *'ălêhem* (*against them*).

just and right on the earth; 3/ that they should circumcise their sons in the covenant that he had made with them; that they should not deviate to the right or left from all the ways that the Lord commanded us; that we should keep ourselves from all sexual impurity and uncleanness; and that we should dismiss all uncleanness and sexual impurity from among us. 4/ If any woman or girl among you commits a sexual offense, burn her in fire; they are not to commit sexual offenses (by) following their eyes and their hearts so that they take wives for themselves from the Canaanite women, because the descendants of Canaan will be uprooted from the earth. 5/ He told them about the punishment of the giants and the punishment of Sodom—how they were condemned because of their wickedness; because of the sexual impurity, uncleanness, and corruption among themselves they died in (their) sexual impurity.[a]

Abraham's Address to His Sons and Grandsons (20:6–10)

6/ "Now you keep yourselves from all sexual impurity and uncleanness and from all the contamination of sin so that you do not make our name into a curse, your entire lives into a (reason for) hissing and all your children into something that is destroyed by the sword. Then you will be accursed like Sodom, and all who remain of you like the people of Gomorrah. 7/ I testify to you my sons: love the God of heaven and hold fast to all his commandments. Do not follow their idols and their uncleanness. 8/ Do not make for yourselves gods that are molten images or statues because they are something empty and have no spirit in them. For they are made by hands, and all who trust in them all trust in nothing at all. Do not worship them or bow to them. 9/ Rather, worship the Most High God and bow to him continually. Look expectantly for his presence at all times, and do what is right and just before him so that he may be delighted with you,

---

[a] The last clause follows Eth; Lat reads *(they) disregarded the commandments* (VanderKam, *The Book of Jubilees* 2.117).

give you his favor, and make the rain to fall for you morning and evening; bless everything that you do—all that you have done on the earth; bless your food and water; and bless the products of your loins, the products of your land, the herds of your cattle, and the flocks of your sheep. 10/ You will be a blessing on the earth, and all the nations of the earth will be delighted with you. They will bless your sons in my name so that they may be blessed as I am."

Abraham Separates His Other Offspring from Isaac and His Sons (20:11–13)

11/ When he had given gifts to Ishmael, his sons, and Keturah's sons and sent them away from his son Isaac, he gave everything to his son Isaac. 12/ Ishmael, his sons, Keturah's sons, and their sons went together and settled from Paran as far as the entrance of Babylon—in all the land toward the east opposite the desert. 13/ They mixed with one another and were called Arabs and Ishmaelites.

Abraham Instructs Isaac (Chapter 21)

Abraham Summons Isaac (21:1a)

21:1a/ In the sixth year of the seventh week of this jubilee [2057] Abraham summoned his son Isaac and gave him orders as follows:

Abraham's Testamentary Instruction of Isaac (21:1b–24)

Abraham's Experience (21:1b–4)

1b/ "I have grown old but do not know when I will die and am satisfied with my days. 2/ Now I am 172[a] years of age. Throughout my entire lifetime I have continually remembered our God and tried to do his will wholeheartedly and to walk a straight course in all his ways. 3/ I have personally hated idols

---

a 4Q219 i:13 preserves the number *-two*; Eth and Lat give his age as *175*.

and despised those who serve them. I have devoted my heart and spirit[a] to keep myself for doing the will of the one who created me. 4/ For he is the living God. He is more holy, faithful, and just than anyone. With him there is no favoritism nor does he accept bribes because he is a just God and one who exercises judgment against all who transgress his commands and despise his covenant.

Abraham's Instructions (21:5–24)

Serve God, Not Idols (21:5)

5/ "Now you, my son, keep his <u>commandments</u>, ordinances, and verdicts. Do not purs<u>ue idols</u>, statues, or molten images.

Priestly Rules (21:6–20)
Prohibition of Eating Blood (21:6)

6/ "<u>Do not</u> eat any blo<u>od of an animal, cattle, or of any bird that</u> flies in the sky.

Sacrificial Procedures (21:7–11)

7/ "If you slaug<u>hter a whole burnt offering or</u>[b] <u>a peace offering that is acceptable, slaughter it and dash their blood on the altar. All the meat of the sacrifice you will offer on the altar with the flour of its grain offering, mixed with</u> oil, with its libation—you will <u>offer it all on the altar as a fire offering, an aroma that is pleasing before God</u>. 8/ As <u>you offer</u> the fat of the pe<u>a</u>ce offering <u>on the fire that is on the altar, you are to remove the fat</u> that is on the intestines and al<u>l the fat that is on the internal organs and the kidneys</u> and <u>all the fat that is on them</u> and that is on the upper thighs <u>and the lobe of the liver with the kidneys</u>. 9/ All of this <u>you will offer</u> as a pleasant fragrance that is acceptable before <u>God, with its sacrifice and its libation as a pleasant fragrance</u>—the <u>f</u>ood of the offering to the Lord. 10/ Eat its meat during <u>that</u> day <u>and on the next day; but</u> the sun is <u>not</u> to <u>s</u>et on it on the next day before

---

a Eth, probably by scribal accident, omits the words read here by Lat: *and despised those who serve them. I have devoted my heart and spirit*.

b The translation follows what appears to be the best reading of 4Q220 1 3 (*Jubilees 1–21*, 622).

it is eaten. It is not to be left over for the third day because it is not acceptable to him. For it was not pleasing and is not therefore commanded. All who eat it will bring guilt on themselves because this is the way I found (it) written in the book of my ancestors, in the words of Enoch and the words of Noah. 11/ On all your offerings you are to place salt; let the covenant of salt not come to an end on any of your sacrifices before the Lord.

Woods Permissible for Burning Sacrifices (21:12–15)

12/ "Be careful about the (kinds of) woods (that are used for) sacrifice so that you bring no (kinds of) woods onto the altar except these only: cypress, silver-fir, almond, fir, pine, cedar, juniper, *date*,[a] olive wood, myrtle, laurel wood, juniper cedar, and balsam. 13/ Of these (kinds of) woods place beneath the sacrifice on the altar ones that have been tested for their appearance. Do not place (beneath it) any split or dark wood; (place there) strong (kinds of) woods and firm ones without any defect—a perfect and new growth. Do not place (there) old wood, for its aroma has left—because there is no longer an aroma upon it as at first. 14/ Apart from these (kinds of) woods there is no other that you are to place (beneath the sacrifice) because their aroma is distinctive and the smell of their aroma goes up to heaven. 15/ Keep this commandment and do it, my son, so that you may behave properly in all your actions.

Cleanliness When Sacrificing (21:16–20)

16/ "At all times be clean in your body. Wash with water before you go to make an offering on the altar. Wash your hands and feet before you approach the sacrifice. When you have finished making an offering, wash your hands and feet again. 17/ No blood is to be visible on you or on your clothing. My son, be careful with blood; be very careful to cover it with dirt. 18/ So you are not to consume blood because the blood is the vital force. Do not consume any blood. 19/ Do not take a bribe for any human blood that will be shed

---

a Charles (*Ethiopic Version*, 75 n. 37) explained the Eth word *tānāk* (apparently a kind of fruit) as a corrupt transcription of a Greek word *phoinix* (*date-palm*).

casually—without punishment—because it is the blood that is shed that makes the earth sin. The earth[a] will not be able to become pure from human blood except through the blood of the one who shed it. 20/ Do not take a bribe or gift for human blood; blood for blood—then it will be acceptable before the Lord, the Most High God. He will be the protection of the good; and (he will be this) so that you may be kept from every evil one and that he may save you from every (kind of) pestilence.[b]

Avoid the Actions of Sinful Humanity (21:21–24)

21/ "I see, my son, that
all the actions of humanity (consist of) sin and wickedness
and all their deeds of impurity, worthlessness, and contamination.
With them there is nothing that is right.
22/ Be careful not to walk in their ways
or tread in their paths
and commit a mortal sin before the Most High God.
Then he will hide his face from you
and will give you over to the power of your offenses.
He will cut you off from the earth
and your descendants from beneath heaven.
Your name and memory[c] will be destroyed from the entire earth.
23/ Depart from all their actions and from all their abominations.
Keep the obligations of the Most High God and do his will.
Then you will be successful in every respect.
24/ He will bless you in all your actions.
He will raise from you a plant of truth in the earth throughout all the generations of the earth.
Then he will not make my name and your name cease from beneath heaven throughout all time.

---

a 4Q219 ii:19 shows that *The earth* is the correct reading; Eth has *blood*.
b 4Q219 ii:22 uses *resheph* meaning *pestilence*; Eth has *death*.
c The two Heb copies for the passage read *memory*, while Eth offers *descendants*.

Abraham Blesses and Dismisses a Joyful Isaac (21:25–26)

25/ "Make your way straight, my son, in peace. May the Most High God—my God and your God—strengthen you to do his will and to bless all your descendants and the remnant of your descendants throughout the generations of eternity with all proper blessings for a blessing throughout the entire earth." 26/ Then he went out from him feeling happy.

Abraham's Last Festival and His Testament to Jacob (Chapter 22)

The Family Celebrates the Festival of Weeks (22:1–6)

22:1/ In the first week in the forty-third[a] jubilee, during the second year [2109]—it was the year in which Abraham died—Isaac and Ishmael came from the well of the oath to their father Abraham to celebrate the Festival of Weeks—this is the Festival of the Firstfruits of the harvest. Abraham was happy that his two sons had come. 2/ For Isaac's possessions in Beersheba were numerous. Isaac used to go and inspect his possessions and then return to his father. 3/ At that time Ishmael came to see his father, and both of them came together. Isaac slaughtered a sacrifice for the offering; he offered (it) on his father's altar that he had made in Hebron. 4/ He sacrificed a peace offering and prepared a joyful feast in front of his brother Ishmael. Rebekah made fresh bread out of new wheat. She gave it to her son Jacob to bring to his father Abraham some of the firstfruits of the land so that he would eat (it) and bless the Creator of everything before he died. 5/ Isaac, too, sent through Jacob his excellent peace offering and wine to his father[b] Abraham for him to eat and drink. 6/ He ate and drank. Then he blessed the Most High God who created the heavens and the earth, who made all the fat things of the earth, and gave them to humanity to eat, drink, and bless their Creator.

---

a Where Eth reads -*fourth* Heb has the correct -*third*.

b The words *his* and *wine to his father* translate Lat; Eth lacks them, probably as a result of scribal error.

Abraham's Prayer (22:7–9)

7/ "Now I pay homage to you, my God, because you have shown me this day. I am now 175 years of age, old and satisfied with (my) days. All of my days have proved to be peace for me. 8/ The enemy's sword has not subdued me in anything at all that you have given me and my sons during all my lifetime until today. 9/ May your kindness and peace rest on your servant and on the descendants of his sons so that they, out of all the nations of the earth, may be your acceptable people and heritage from now until all the time of the earth's history throughout all ages."

Abraham Prays for Jacob (22:10–15)

10/ He summoned Jacob and said to him, "My son Jacob, may the God of all bless and strengthen you to do before him what is right and what he wills. May he choose you and your descendants to be his people for his heritage in accord with his will throughout all time. Now you, my son Jacob, come close and kiss me." 11/ So he came close and kissed him. Then he said, "May my son Jacob and all his sons be blessed to the Most High God throughout all ages. May the Lord give you righteous descendants, and may he sanctify some of your sons in the entire earth. May the nations serve you, and may all the nations bow before your descendants. 12/ Be strong before people and exercise power among all of Seth's descendants. Then your ways and the ways of your sons will be justified so that they may be a holy people. 13/ May the Most High God give you all the blessings with which he blessed me and with which he blessed Noah and Adam. May they come to rest on the sacred head of your descendants throughout each and every generation and forever. 14/ May he purify you from all filthy pollution so that you may be pardoned for every sin you have committed in ignorance. May he strengthen and bless you; may you possess the entire earth. 15/ May he renew his covenant with you so that you may be for him the people of his heritage throughout all ages. May he truly and

Abraham Gives Commands to Jacob (22:16–24)

16/ "Now you, my son Jacob,
remember what I say
and keep the commandments of your father Abraham.
Separate from the nations,
and do not eat with them.
Do not act as they do,
and do not become their companion,
for their actions are something that is impure,
and all their ways are defiled and something abominable
and detestable.
17/ They offer their sacrifices to the dead,
and they worship demons.
They eat in tombs,
and everything they do is empty and worthless.
18/ They have no mind to think,
and their eyes do not see what they do
and how they err in saying to (a piece of) wood,
'You are my god';
or to a stone,
'You are my lord;
you are my deliverer.'
They have no mind."

19/ "As for you, my son Jacob,
may the Most High God help you
and the God of heaven[a] bless you.

"May he remove you from their impurity and from all their error. 20/ Be careful, my son Jacob, not to marry a woman from all the descendants of Canaan's daughters, because all of his descendants are (meant) for being uprooted from the earth. 21/ For through Ham's sin Canaan erred. All of his descendants and all of his (people) who remain will be

---

a Lat reads the letters *adae* that may be left from an original *saddae* (*shadday*).

destroyed from the earth; on the day of judgment there will be no one (descended) from him who will be saved. 22/ There is no hope in the land of the living for all who worship idols and for those who are odious. For they will descend to Sheol and will go to the place of judgment. There will be no memory of any of them on the earth. As the people of Sodom were taken from the earth, so all who worship idols will be destroyed.[a]

23/ Do not be afraid, my son Jacob,
and do not be upset, son of Abraham.
May the Most High God keep you from corruption;
and from every erroneous way may he rescue you.

24/ "This house I have built for myself to put my name on it upon the earth. It has been given to you and to your descendants forever. It will be called Abraham's house. It has been given to you and your descendants forever because you will build my house and will establish my name before God until eternity. Your descendants and your name will remain throughout all the history of the earth."

Abraham and Jacob Lie Down Together (22:25–26)

25/ Then he finished commanding and blessing him. 26/ The two of them lay down together on one bed. Jacob slept in the bosom of his grandfather Abraham. He kissed him seven times, and his feelings and mind were happy about him.

Abraham Blesses the Sleeping Jacob (22:27–30)

27/ He blessed him wholeheartedly and said: "The Most High God is the God of all and Creator of everything who brought me from Ur of the Chaldeans to give me this land in order that I should possess it forever and raise up holy descendants so that they may be blessed forever." 28/ Then he blessed Jacob: "My son, with whom I am *exceedingly* happy[b] with all

---

a 4Q221 2 i:3 reads *destroyed* where Eth has *taken*.
b For the difficulties with the Eth here, see *Jubilees 22–50*, 651.

my mind and feelings—may your grace and mercy continue on him and his descendants for all time. 29/ Do not leave or neglect him from now until the time of eternity. May your eyes be open on him and his descendants so that they may watch over them and so that you may bless and sanctify them as the people of your heritage. 30/ Bless him with all your blessings from now until all the time of eternity. With your entire will renew your covenant and your grace with him and with his descendants throughout all the generations of the earth."

Abraham's Death and the Pattern of Human Life Spans (Chapter 23)

The Death of Abraham (23:1–7)

23:1/ He put two of Jacob's fingers on his eyes and blessed the God of gods. He covered his face, stretched out his feet, fell asleep forever, and was gathered to his ancestors. 2/ During all of this Jacob was lying in his bosom and was unaware that his grandfather Abraham had died. 3/ When Jacob awakened from his sleep, there was Abraham cold as ice. He said, "Father, father!" But he said nothing to him. Then he knew that he was dead. 4/ He got up from his bosom and ran and told his mother Rebekah. Rebekah went to Isaac at night and told him. They went together—and Jacob with them (carrying) a lamp in his hands. When they came they found Abraham's corpse lying (there). 5/ Isaac fell on his father's face, cried, and kissed him. 6/ After the report was heard in the household of Abraham, his son Ishmael set out and came to his father Abraham. He mourned for his father Abraham— he and all the men of Abraham's household. They mourned very much. 7/ They—both of his sons Isaac and Ishmael— buried him in the cave of Machpelah near his wife Sarah. All the people of his household as well as Isaac, Ishmael, and all their sons and Keturah's sons in their places mourned for him for 40 days. Then the tearful mourning for Abraham was completed.

The Pattern of Human Life Spans (23:8–31)

Abraham's Short Life in a Period of Decreasing Longevity (23:8–10)

8/ He had lived for three jubilees and four weeks of years—175 years—when he completed his lifetime. He had grown old and was satisfied with (his) days. 9/ For the times of the ancients were 19 jubilees for their lifetimes. After the flood they started to decrease from 19 jubilees,[a] to be fewer with respect to jubilees, to age quickly, and to have their times be completed because of the numerous difficulties and through the wickedness of their ways—with the exception of Abraham. 10/ For Abraham was perfect with the Lord in everything that he did—being properly pleasing throughout all his lifetime. And yet (even) he had not completed four jubilees during his lifetime by the time he became old—because of wickedness—and reached the end of his time.

Continual Decline in Life Spans (23:11–15)

11/ All the generations that will come into being from now until the great day of judgment[b] will grow old quickly—before they complete two jubilees. It will be their knowledge that will leave them because of their old age; all of their knowledge will depart. 12/ In those days, if a man lives a jubilee and one-half of years, it will be said about him: "He has lived for a long time." But the greater part of his time will be (characterized by) difficulties, toil, and distress without peace 13/ because (there will be) blow upon blow, trouble upon trouble, distress upon distress, bad news upon bad news, disease upon disease, and every (kind of) bad punishment like this, one with the other: disease and stomach pains; snow,

---

a Lat lacks *to decrease from 19 jubilees*, while the expression is present in Eth. It is difficult to decide whether Lat omitted it or Eth has a reading that somewhat duplicates what follows.

b Most Eth mss read *the great day of judgment*, but a few of them and Lat have *the day of the great judgment*.

hail, and frost; fever, cold, and numbness; famine, death, sword, captivity, and every (sort of) blow and difficulty.[a] 14/ All of this will happen to the evil generation that makes the earth commit sin[b] through sexual impurity, contamination, and their detestable actions. 15/ Then it will be said: "The days of the ancients were numerous—as many as 1,000 years—and good. But now the days of our lives, if a man has lived for a long time, are 70 years, and, if he is strong, 80 years." All are evil and there is no peace during the days of that evil generation.

Low Point in the Time of the Evil Generation (23:16–25)

16/ During that generation the children will find fault with their fathers and elders because of sin and injustice, because of what they say and the great evils that they commit, and because of their abandoning the covenant that the Lord had made between them and himself so that they should observe and perform all his commands, ordinances, and all his laws without deviating to the left or right. 17/ For all have acted wickedly; every mouth speaks what is sinful. Everything that they do is impure and something detestable; all their ways are (characterized by) contamination, impurity, and destruction. 18/ The earth will indeed be destroyed because of all that they do. There will be no produce, wine, or oil because what they do (constitutes) complete apostasy. All will be destroyed together—animals, cattle, birds, and all fish of the sea—because of humanity. 19/ One group will struggle with another—the young with the old, the old with the young; the poor with the rich, the lowly with the great; and the needy with the ruler—regarding the law and the covenant. For they have forgotten commandment, covenant, festival, month, Sabbath, jubilee, and every verdict. 20/ They will stand up

---

a For issues connected with the nouns in v 13 and the variant readings in the mss and copies, see *Jubilees 22–50*, 672–73.

b Some Eth copies read (*makes*) *the earth commit sin*, while Lat has *commits sin on the earth*.

with swords[a] and warfare in order to bring them back to the way; but they will not be brought back until much blood is shed on the earth by each group.

21/ Those who escape will not turn from their wickedness to the right way because all of them will elevate themselves for (the purpose of) cheating and through wealth so that one takes everything that belongs to another. They will mention the great name but neither truly nor rightly. They will defile the holy things of the holy one with the impure corruption of their contamination. 22/ There will be great anger from the Lord for the actions of that generation. He will deliver them to the sword, judgment, captivity, plundering, and devouring. 23/ He will arouse against them the sinful nations who will have no mercy or kindness for them and who will show partiality to no one, whether old or young, or anyone at all, because they are evil and strong so that they are more evil than all humanity. They will cause chaos in Israel and sin against Jacob. Much blood will be shed on the earth, and there will be no one who gathers up (corpses) or who buries (them).

24/ At that time they will cry out and call and pray to be rescued from the power of the sinful nations, but there will be no one who rescues (them). 25/ The children's heads will turn white with gray hair. A child who is three weeks of age will look old like one whose years are 100, and their condition will be destroyed through distress and pain.

The Children and the Reversal in Longevity (23:26–31)

26/ In those days the children will begin to study the laws, to seek out the commands, and to return to the right way. 27/ The days will begin to become numerous and increase, and humanity as well—generation by generation and day by day until their lifetimes approach 1,000 years and to more years than the number of days (had been). 28/ There will be no old man, nor anyone who has lived out (his) lifetime, because all

---

a Lat reads *with bow and with swords*.

of them will be infants and children. 29/ They will complete and live their entire lifetimes peacefully and joyfully. There will be neither a satan nor any evil one who will destroy. For their entire lifetimes will be times of blessing and healing.

30/ Then the Lord will heal his servants. They will rise and see great peace. He will expel his enemies. The righteous will see (this), offer praise, and be very happy forever and ever. <u>They will see all</u> their punishments and <u>curses on</u> their enemies. 31/ Their bones will rest in the earth and <u>their spirits will</u> be very happy. They will know that <u>there is a God who executes</u> judgment but shows kindness <u>to</u> hundred<u>s and tens of thou</u>sands and to all who love him.

Command That Moses Write the Message (23:32)

32/ Now you, Moses, write down these words because this is how it is written and entered in the testimony of the heavenly tablets for the history of eternity.

Isaac and the Philistines (Chapter 24)

Narrative Setting (24:1–2)

24:1/ After Abraham's death, the Lord blessed his son Isaac. He set out from Hebron and went and lived during the first year of the third week of this jubilee [2073] at the well of the vision for seven years. 2/ During the first year of the fourth week [2080] a famine—different than the first famine that had occurred in Abraham's lifetime—began in the land.

Jacob Gains the Right of Firstborn (24:3–7)

3/ When Jacob was cooking lentil porridge, Esau came hungry from the field. He said to his brother Jacob, "Give me some of this *red*[a] porridge." But Jacob said to him, "Hand over to

---

a Eth reads *wheat*, a mistake that, as Dillmann ("Jubiläen," 71 n. 23) observed, arose when Greek *pyrou* (*of wheat*) was translated rather than the correct *pyrrou* (*red*); see Gen 25:30.

me your birthright that belongs to the firstborn, and then I will give you food and some of this porridge as well." 4/ Esau said to himself, "I will die. What good will this right of the firstborn do?" So he said to Jacob, "I (hereby) give (it) to you." 5/ Jacob said to him, "Swear to me today." So he swore to him. 6/ Then Jacob gave the food and porridge to his brother Esau, and he ate until he was full. Esau repudiated the right of the firstborn. This is why he was named Esau and Edom: because of the *red* porridge that Jacob gave him in exchange for his right of the firstborn. 7/ So Jacob became the older one, but Esau was lowered from his prominent position.

Famine, Journey to Gerar, Blessing (24:8–11)

8/ As there was a famine over the land, Isaac set out to go down to Egypt during the second year of this week [2081]. He went to Gerar to the Philistine king Abimelech. 9/ The Lord appeared to him and told him, "Do not go down to Egypt. Stay in the land that I will tell you. Live as a foreigner in this land. I will be with you and bless you, 10/ because I will give this entire land to you and your descendants. I will carry out the terms of my oath that I swore to your father Abraham. I will make your descendants as numerous as the stars of the sky. I will give this entire land to your descendants. 11/ All the peoples of the earth will be blessed through your descendants because of the fact that your father obeyed me and kept my obligations, commands, laws, statutes, and covenant. Now obey me and live in this land."

Isaac in Gerar (24:12–17)

12/ He lived in Gerar for three weeks of years. 13/ Abimelech gave orders as follows regarding him and everything that belonged to him: "Anyone who touches him or anything that belongs to him is to die." 14/ Isaac prospered among the Philistines and possessed much property: cattle, sheep, camels, donkeys, and much property.[a] 15/ He planted seeds in the land of the Philistines, and he harvested one hundredfold. When Isaac had become very great, the Philistines grew jealous of him. 16/ (As for) all the wells that Abraham's servants had dug during Abraham's lifetime—the Philistines covered them up after Abraham's death and filled them with dirt. 17/ Then Abimelech told Isaac, "Leave us because you have become much too great for us." So Isaac left that place during the first year of the seventh week [2102]. He lived as a foreigner in the valleys of Gerar.

Isaac and His Wells in the Valleys of Gerar (24:18–20)

18/ They again dug the water wells which the servants of his father Abraham had dug and the Philistines had covered up after his father Abraham's death. He called them by the names that his father Abraham had given them. 19/ Isaac's servants dug wells in the wadi and found flowing water. Then the shepherds of Gerar quarreled with Isaac's shepherds and said, "This water is ours." So Isaac named that well Difficult "because they have been difficult for us." 20/ They dug a second well, and they fought about it too. He named it Hostility.[b] When he had set out, they dug another well but did not quarrel about it. He named it Wide. Isaac said, "Now the Lord has enlarged (a place) for us, and we have increased in numbers on the land."

Blessing and Sacrifice in Beersheba (24:21–23)

21/ He went up from there to the well of the oath during the first year of the first week in the forty-fourth jubilee [2108]. 22/ The Lord appeared to him that night—on the first of the first month—and said to him, "I am the God of your father Abraham. Do not be afraid because I am with you and will

---

a Lat has *and many servants*.

b Eth reads *narrow*, possibly to furnish an antonym to the name of the next well. See Gen 26:21.

bless you. I will certainly make your descendants as numerous as the sand of the earth for the sake of my servant Abraham." 23/ There he built the altar that his father Abraham had first built. He called on the Lord's name and offered a sacrifice to the God of his father Abraham.

Isaac's Oath with the Philistines and Curse upon Them (24:24–33)

24/ They dug a well and found flowing water. 25/ But when Isaac's servants dug another well, they did not find water. They went and told Isaac that they had not found water. Isaac said, "On this very day I have sworn[a] an oath to the Philistines; now this has happened to us." 26/ He named that place the well of the oath because there he had sworn an oath to Abimelech, his companion Ahuzzath, and his guard Phicol. 27/ On that day Isaac realized that he had sworn an oath to them under pressure to make peace with them. 28/ On that day Isaac cursed the Philistines and said, "May the Philistines be cursed from among all peoples at the day of anger and wrath. May the Lord make them into (an object of) disgrace and a curse, into (an object of) anger and wrath in the hands of the sinful nations and in the hands of the Kittim. 29/ Whoever escapes from the enemy's sword and from the Kittim may the just nation in judgment eradicate from beneath the sky, for they will become enemies and opponents to my sons during their times on the earth. 30/ They will have no one left or anyone who is rescued on the day of judgmental anger, for all the descendants of the Philistines (are meant) for destruction, eradication, and removal from the earth. All of Caphtor will no longer have either name or descendants left upon the earth.
31/ For even if he should go up to the sky,
from there he would come down;
even if he should become powerful on the earth,[b]
from there he will be torn out.
Even if he should hide himself among the nations,

---

a Lat places *because* before *I have sworn*.
b For this line Lat has *where(ver) he would flee*.

from there he will be uprooted;
even if he should go down to Sheol,
there his punishment will increase.
There he will have no peace.
32/ Even if he should go into captivity through the power
    of those who seek his life,
they will kill him along the way.
There will remain for him neither name nor descendants on
    the entire earth,
because he is going to an eternal curse."

33/ This is the way it has been written and inscribed regarding him on the heavenly tablets—to do (this) to him on the day of judgment so that he may be eradicated from the earth.

Rebekah and Jacob (Chapter 25)

Dialogue between Rebekah and Jacob (25:1–10)

Rebekah Instructs Jacob about a Fitting Marriage Partner (25:1–3)

25:1/ In the second year of this week, in this jubilee [2109], Rebekah summoned her son Jacob and spoke to him: "My son, do not marry any of the Canaanite women like your brother Esau who has married two wives from the descendants of Canaan. They have embittered my life with all the impure things that they do because everything that they do (consists of) sexual impurity and lewdness. They have no decency because (what they do) is evil. 2/ I, my son, love you very much; my heart and my affection bless you at all times of the day and watches of the nights. 3/ Now, my son, listen to me. Do as your mother wishes. Do not marry any of the women of this land but (someone) from my[a] father's house and from my father's clan. Marry someone from my father's house. The Most High God will bless you; your family will be a righteous family and your descendants (will be) holy."

---

a Many Eth mss read *your* here and in the next expression.

Jacob Explains His Behavior and View of Marriage (25:4–10)

4/ Then Jacob spoke with his mother Rebekah and said to her, "Mother, I am now nine weeks of years [= 63 years] and have known no woman. I have neither touched (one) nor have I even considered marrying any woman of all the descendants of Canaan's daughters. 5/ For I recall, mother, what our father Abraham ordered me—that I should not marry anyone from all the descendants of Canaan's house. For I will marry (someone) from the descendants of my father's house and from my family. 6/ Earlier I heard, mother, that daughters had been born to your brother Laban. I have set my mind on them for the purpose of marrying one of them. 7/ For this reason I have kept myself from sinning and from becoming corrupted in any ways during my entire lifetime because father Abraham gave me many orders about lewdness and sexual impurity. 8/ Despite everything he ordered me, my brother has been quarreling with me for the last 22 years and has often said to me, 'My brother, marry one of the sisters of my two wives.' But I have not been willing to do as he did. 9/ I swear in your presence, mother, that during my entire lifetime I will not marry any of the descendants of Canaan's daughters nor will I do what is wrong as my brother Esau[a] has done. 10/ Do not be afraid, mother, and be assured that I will do as you wish. I will behave rightly and will never conduct myself corruptly."

Rebekah Blesses God and Prays for Jacob (25:11–23)

11/ Then she lifted her face to heaven, extended her fingers, and opened her mouth. She blessed the Most High God who had created the heavens and the earth and gave him thanks and praise. 12/ She said, "May the Lord God be blessed, and may his name be blessed forever and ever—he who gave me Jacob, a pure son and a holy offspring, for he belongs to you. May his descendants be yours throughout all time, through-

---

a The Eth copies lack the name but 4Q222 1 2 has it.

out the history of eternity. 13/ Bless him, Lord, and place a righteous blessing in my mouth so that I may bless him." 14/ At that time the spirit of righteousness descended into her mouth. She put her two hands on Jacob's head and said:
15/ "Blessed are you, righteous Lord, God of the ages;
and may he bless you more than all the human race.
My son, may he provide the right path for you
and reveal what is right to your descendants.
16/ May he multiply your sons during your lifetime;
may they rise in number to the months of the year.
May their children be more numerous and great than the stars of the sky;
may their number be larger than the sands of the sea.
17/ May he give them this pleasant land
as he said he would give it for all time
to Abraham and his descendants after him;
may they own it as an eternal possession.
18/ Son, may I see your blessed children during my lifetime;
may all your descendants be blessed and holy descendants.
19/ As you have given rest to your mother's spirit during her lifetime,
so may the womb of the one who gave birth to you bless you.
My affection and my breasts bless you;
my mouth and my tongue praise you greatly.
20/ Increase and spread out in the land;
may your descendants be perfect throughout all eternity
in the joy of heaven and earth.
May your descendants be delighted,
and, on the great day of peace, may they have peace.
21/ May your name and your descendants continue until all ages.
May the Most High God be their God;
may the righteous God live with them;
and may his sanctuary be built among them into all ages.
22/ May the one who blesses you be blessed
and anyone who curses you falsely be cursed.

23/ She then kissed him and said to him, "May the eternal Lord love you as your mother's heart and her affection are delighted with you and bless you." She then stopped blessing (him).

Jacob, Not Esau, Receives Isaac's Blessing (Chapter 26)
Isaac's Instructions to Esau (26:1–2)

26:1/ During the seventh year of this week [2114] Isaac summoned his older son Esau and said to him, "My son, I have grown old and now have difficulty seeing, but I do not know when I will die. 2/ Now then, take your hunting gear—your quiver and your bow—and go to the field. Hunt on my behalf and catch (something) for me, my son. Then prepare (some) food for me just as I like (it) and bring (it) to me so that I may eat (it) and bless you before I die."

Rebekah and Jacob (26:3–9)

Rebekah's Plan (26:3–6)

3/ Rebekah was listening as Isaac was talking to Esau. 4/ When Esau went out early to the open country to trap (something), catch (it), and bring (it) to his father, 5/ Rebekah summoned her son Jacob and said to him, "I have just heard your father Isaac saying to your brother Esau, 'Trap (something) for me, prepare me (some) food, bring (it) to me, and let me eat (it). Then I will bless you in the Lord's presence before I die.' 6/ Now, therefore, listen, my son, to what I am ordering you. Go to your flock and take for me two excellent kids. Let me prepare them as food for your father just as he likes (it). You are to take (it) to your father, and he is to eat it so that he may bless you in the Lord's presence before he dies and you may be blessed."

Jacob's Reply and Rebekah's Insistence (26:7–9)

7/ But Jacob said to his mother Rebekah, "Mother, I will not be sparing about anything that my father eats and that pleases him, but I am afraid, mother, that he will recognize my voice and wish to touch me. 8/ You know that I am smooth while my brother Esau is hairy. I will look to him like a mocker. I would be doing something that he did not order me[a] (to do), and he would get angry at me. Then I would bring a curse on myself, not a blessing." 9/ But his mother Rebekah said to him, "Let your curse be on me, my son; just obey me."

Isaac's Unwitting Blessing of Jacob (26:10–25ab)

10/ So Jacob obeyed his mother Rebekah. He went and took two excellent, fat kids and brought them to his mother. His mother prepared them as he liked (them). 11/ Rebekah then took her older son Esau's favorite clothes that were present with her in the house. She dressed her younger son Jacob (in them) and placed the goatskins on his forearms and on the exposed parts of his neck. 12/ She then put the food and bread that she had prepared in her son Jacob's hand. 13/ He went in to his father and said, "I am your son. I have done as you told me. Get up, have a seat, and eat some of what I have caught, father, so that you may bless me." 14/ Isaac said to his son, "How have you managed to find (it) so quickly, my son?" 15/ Jacob said, "It was your God who made me find[b] (it) in front of me." 16/ Then Isaac said to him, "Come close and let me touch you, my son, (so that I can tell) whether you are my son Esau or not." 17/ Jacob came close to his father Isaac. When he touched him he said, 18/ "The voice is Jacob's voice, but the forearms are Esau's forearms." He did not recognize him because there was a turn of affairs from heaven to distract his mind. Isaac did not recognize (him) because his forearms were hairy like Esau's forearms so that he should bless him. 19/ He said, "Are you my son Esau?" He said, "I am your son." Then he said, "Bring (it) to me and let me eat some of what you have caught, my son, so that I may

---

a At *he did not order me*, Lat reads *his counsel/advice* (VanderKam, *Book of Jubilees* 2:164).

b Rather than *made me find*, Lat reads *guided*.

bless you." 20/ He then brought him (food) and he ate; he brought him wine and he drank.

21/ His father Isaac said to him, "Come close and kiss me, my son." He came close and kissed him. 22/ When he smelled the fragrant aroma of his clothes, he blessed him and said, "Indeed the aroma of my son is like the aroma of a full[a] field that the Lord has blessed.
23/ May the Lord grant to you and multiply for you
(your share) of the dew of heaven and the dew of the earth;
may he multiply grain and oil for you.
May the nations serve you,
and the peoples bow to you.
24/ Become lord of your brothers;[b]
may the sons of your mother bow to you.
May all the blessings with which the Lord has blessed me
    and blessed my father Abraham
belong to you and your descendants forever.
May the one who curses you be cursed,
and the one who blesses you be blessed."

25ab/ After Isaac had finished blessing his son Jacob and Jacob had left his father Isaac, he hid

Isaac and Esau (26:25c–34)

25c/ and his brother Esau arrived from his hunting. 26/ He, too, prepared food and brought (it) to his father. He said to his father, "Let my father rise and eat some of what I have caught and so that you may bless me." 27/ His father Isaac said to him, "Who are you?" He said to him, "I am your firstborn, your son Esau. I have done as you ordered me." 28/ Then Isaac was absolutely dumbfounded and said, "Who was the one who hunted, caught (something) for me, and brought (it)? I ate some of everything before you came and blessed

---

    a Eth lacks *full*, but Lat, with SP LXX OL Gen 27:27, reads the adjective.

    b The pl. *brothers* is the preferred reading, but many Eth mss with LXX OL Eth Gen 27:29 have *brother* since Jacob had only one brother.

him. He and all his descendants are to be blessed forever." 29/ When Esau heard what his father Isaac said, he cried out very loudly and bitterly and said to his father, "Bless me too, father!" 30/ He said to him, "Your brother came deceptively and took your blessings." He said, "Now I know the reason why he was named Jacob. This is now the second time that he has cheated me. The first time he took my birthright and now he has taken my blessing." 31/ He said, "Have you not saved a blessing for me, father?" Isaac said in reply to Esau, "I have just now designated him as your lord. I have given him all his brothers to be his servants. I have strengthened him with an abundance of grain, wine, and oil. So, what shall I now do for you, my son?" 32/ Esau said to his father Isaac, "Do you have just one blessing, father? Bless me too, father!" Then Esau cried loudly. 33/ Isaac said in reply to him, "The place where you live is indeed to be (away) from the dew of the earth and from the dew of heaven above. 34/ You will live by your sword and will serve your brother. May it be that, if you become great and remove his yoke from your neck, then you will commit an offense fully worthy of death and your descendants will be eradicated from beneath the sky."

Esau's Plot to Kill Jacob (26:35)

35/ Esau kept threatening Jacob because of the blessing with which his father had blessed him. He said to himself, "The time of mourning for my father is now approaching. Then I will kill my brother Jacob."

Jacob Leaves Home and Encounters the Lord in Bethel (Chapter 27)

Rebekah and Jacob Discuss Plans (27:1–7)

27:1/ Rebekah was told in a dream what her older son Esau had said. So Rebekah sent and summoned her younger son Jacob and said to him, 2/ "Your brother Esau will now try to get revenge against you by killing you. 3/ So then, my son, listen to me.

Set out and run away to my brother Laban—to Haran. Stay with him for a few days until your brother's anger turns away and he stops being angry at you and forgets everything that you have done to him. Then I will send and take you back from there." 4/ Jacob said, "I am not afraid. If he wishes to kill me, I will kill him." 5/ She said to him, "May I not lose my two sons in one day." 6/ Jacob said to his mother Rebekah, "You are of course aware that my father has grown old, and I notice that he has difficulty seeing. If I left him, he would consider it a bad thing be<u>cause I would be leaving</u> him and going away from you. My father would be angry and curse me. <u>I will</u> <u>not go</u>. <u>If he</u> sends me, only then will I go." 7/ Rebekah said to Jacob, "I will go in and te<u>ll him</u>. Then he will send you."

Isaac Carries Out Rebekah's Instructions and Blesses Jacob (27:8–11)

8/ Rebekah went in and said to Isaac, "I despise my life because of the two Hittite women whom Esau has married. If Jacob marries one of the women of the land who are like them, why should I remain alive any longer, because the Canaanite women are evil." 9/ So Isaac summoned his son Jacob, blessed and instructed him, and said to him, 10/ "Do not marry any of the Canaanite women. Set out, go to Mesopotamia, to the house of Bethuel, your mother's father. From there take a wife from the daughters of Laban, your mother's brother. 11/ May the God of Shaddai bless you; may he make you increase, become numerous, and be a throng of nations. May he give the blessings of my father Abraham to you and to your descendants after you so that you may possess the land where you wander as a foreigner—and all the land that the Lord gave to Abraham. Have a safe trip, my son."

Jacob Leaves and His Parents Cope (27:12–18)

12/ So Isaac sent Jacob away. He went to Mesopotamia, to Laban, the son of Bethuel the Aramean—the brother of Rebekah,

Jacob's mother. 13/ After Jacob had set out to go to Mesopotamia, Rebekah grieved for her son and kept crying. 14/ Isaac said to Rebekah, "My sister, do not cry for my son Jacob because he will go safely and return safely. 15/ The Most High God will guard him from every evil and will be with him because he will not abandon him throughout his entire lifetime. 16/ For I well know that his ways will be directed favorably wherever he goes until he returns safely to us and we see that he is safe. 17/ Do not be afraid for him, my sister, because he is just in his way.[a] He is perfect; he is a true man. He will not be abandoned. Do not cry." 18/ So Isaac was consoling Rebekah regarding her son Jacob, and he blessed him.

The Theophany at Luz/Bethel (27:19-27)

19/ Jacob left the well of the oath to go to Haran during the first year of the second week of the forty-fourth jubilee [2115]. He arrived at Luz that is on the mountain—that is, Bethel—on the first of the first month of this week. He arrived at the place in the evening, turned off the road to the west of the highway during this night, and slept there because the sun had set. 20/ He took one of the stones of that place and set it at the place (for) his head[b] beneath that tree. He was traveling alone and fell asleep. 21/ That night he dreamed that a ladder was set up on the earth and its top was reaching heaven; that angels of the Lord were going up and down on it; and that the Lord was standing[c] on it. 22/ He spoke with Jacob and said, "I am the God of Abraham your father and the God of Isaac. The land on which you are sleeping I will give to you and your descendants after you. 23/ Your descendants will be like the sands of the earth. You will become numerous toward the west, the east, the north, and the south. All the

---

a Lat reads *he is on/in the right way*.

b Eth lacks *at the place (for) his head*, but Lat has it and 1Q17 5 has space for it (as in Gen 28:11). Eth supplies the phrase at 27:26.

c Lat has *sitting*; cf. LXX Gen 28:13.

families of the nations[a] will be blessed through you and your descendants. 24/ As for me, I will be with you. I will guard you wherever you go. I will bring you back safely to this land because I will not abandon you until I have done everything that I have said to you." 25/ Jacob said in (his) sleep: "This place is indeed the house of the Lord but I did not know (it)." He was afraid and said, "This place, which is nothing but the house of the Lord, is awe-inspiring; and this is the gate of heaven."

26/ Jacob, upon arising early in the morning, took the stone that he had placed at his head and set it up as a pillar for a marker. He poured oil on top of it and named that place Bethel. But at first the name of this area was Luz. 27/ Jacob vowed to the Lord, "If the Lord is with me and guards me on this road on which I am traveling and gives me food to eat and clothes to wear so that I return safely to my father's house, then the Lord will be my God. Also, this stone that I have set up as a pillar for a marker in this place is to become the house of the Lord. All that you have given me I will indeed tithe to you, my God."

Jacob Gains a Family and Acquires Wealth (Chapter 28)

Marriages and the Law of the Firstborn Daughter (28:1-10)

28:1/ He set out on foot and went to the eastern land, to Laban, Rebekah's brother. He remained with him and served him in exchange for his daughter Rachel for one week. 2/ During the first year of the third week [2122] he said to him, "Give me my wife for whom I have served you seven years." Laban said to Jacob, "I will give you your wife." 3/ Laban prepared a banquet, took his older daughter Leah, and gave (her) to Jacob as a wife. He gave her Zilpah, his servant girl, as a maid. But Jacob was not aware (of this) because Jacob thought she was Rachel. 4/ He went in to her, and, to his surprise, she was Leah. Jacob was angry at Laban and said to him, "Why

---

a Lat reads *earth*, with Gen 28:14.

have you acted this way? Was it not for Rachel that I served you and not for Leah? Why have you wronged me? Take your daughter and I will go because you have done a bad thing to me." 5/ For Jacob loved Rachel more than Leah because Leah's eyes were weak, though her figure was very lovely; but Rachel's eyes were beautiful, her figure was lovely, and she was very pretty. 6/ Laban said to Jacob, "It is not customary in our country to give the younger daughter before the older one." It is not right to do this because this is the way it is ordained and written on the heavenly tablets: that no one should give his younger daughter before his older one, but he should first give the older and after her the younger. Regarding the man who acts in this way they enter a sin in heaven.[a] There is no one who is just and does this because this action is evil in the Lord's presence. 7/ Now you order the Israelites not to do this. They are neither to take nor give the younger before giving precedence to the older because it is very wicked. 8/ Laban said to Jacob, "Let the seven days of the banquet for this one go by; then I will give you Rachel so that you serve me a second (term of) seven years by tending my flocks as you did during the first week." 9/ At the time when the seven days of Leah's banquet had passed by, Laban gave Rachel to Jacob so that he would serve him a second (term of) seven years. He gave her Bilhah, Zilpah's sister, as a maid. 10/ He served seven years a second time for Rachel because Leah had been given to him for nothing.

The Births of Twelve Children (28:11–24)

11/ When the Lord opened Leah's womb, she became pregnant and gave birth to a son for Jacob. He named him Reuben on the fourteenth day of the ninth month during the first year of the third week [2122]. 12/ Now Rachel's womb was closed because the Lord saw that Leah was hated but Rachel was loved. 13/ Jacob again went in to Leah. She became pregnant and gave birth to a second son for Jacob. He named

---

a Several excellent mss read *the tablets of heaven*.

him Simeon on the twenty-first of the tenth month, during the third year of this week [2124]. 14/ Jacob again went in to Leah. She became pregnant and gave birth to a third son for him. He named him Levi on the first of the first month during the sixth year of this week [2127]. 15/ He went in yet another time to her and she gave birth to a fourth son. He named him Judah on the fifteenth of the third month during the first year of the fourth week [2129].

16/ Throughout all this Rachel was jealous of Leah, since she was not bearing children. She said to Jacob, "Give me children." Jacob said to her, "Have I withheld the product of your womb from you? Have I abandoned you?" 17/ When Rachel saw that Leah had given birth to four sons for Jacob—Reuben, Simeon, Levi, and Judah—she said to him, "Go in to my servant girl Bilhah. Then she will become pregnant and give birth to a son for me." 18/ So he went in,[a] she became pregnant, and gave birth to a son for him. He named him Dan on the ninth of the sixth month during the sixth year of the third week [2127]. 19/ Jacob once again went in to Bilhah. She became pregnant and gave birth to a second son for Jacob. Rachel named him Naphtali on the fifth of the seventh month during the second year of the fourth week [2130]. 20/ When Leah saw that she had become barren[b] and was not bearing children, she grew jealous of Rachel and also gave her maid Zilpah to Jacob as a wife. She became pregnant and gave birth to a son. Leah named him Gad on the twelfth of the eighth month during the third year of the fourth week [2131].[c] 21/ He again went in to her, and she became pregnant and gave birth to a second son for him. Leah named him Asher on the second of the eleventh month during the fifth year of the fourth week [2133]. 22/ Then

---

a For the clause Lat has *She gave her servant girl Bilhah as a wife*. Both expressions appear in Gen 30:4.

b Lat *was held back*. See *Jubilees 22–50*, 775.

c For issues with the date in Lat here and the ones that follow, see *Jubilees 22–50*, 775–76.

Jacob went in to Leah. She became pregnant and gave birth to a son for Jacob. He named him Issachar on the fourth (day) of the fifth month during the fourth year of the fourth week [2132]. She gave him to a nurse. 23/ Again Jacob went in to her. She became pregnant and gave birth to twins: a son and a daughter. She named the son Zebulun and the daughter Dinah on the seventh (of the) seventh month, during the sixth year, the fourth week [2134]. 24/ Then the Lord was kind to Rachel. He opened her womb, and she became pregnant and gave birth to a son. She named him Joseph on the first of the fourth month, during the sixth year in this fourth week [2134].

Jacob's Work for Laban (28:25–30)

25/ At the time when Joseph was born, Jacob said to Laban, "Give me my wives and my children so that I may go to my father Isaac and make a house for myself, because I have completed the years during which I served you in exchange for your two daughters. Then I will go to my father's house." 26/ Laban said to Jacob, "Stay with me[a] in exchange for your wages. Tend my flocks for me again and take your wages." 27/ They agreed among themselves that he would give him his wages: all the lambs and kids that were born a dark gray color and dark mixed with white were to be his wages. 28/ All the dark-colored sheep kept giving birth to all with variously colored spots of every kind and various shades of dark gray. The sheep would again give birth to (lambs) that looked like them. All with spots belonged to Jacob and those without spots to Laban. 29/ Jacob's possessions grew very large; he acquired cattle, sheep, donkeys, camels, and male and female servants. 30/ When Laban and his sons became jealous of Jacob, Laban took back his sheep from him and kept his eye on him for evil purposes.

---

a Lat has *Wait for me*. See *Jubilees 22–50*, 776.

Jacob Leaves Haran and Deals with Laban, Esau, and His Parents (Chapter 29)

Jacob and His Family Leave Laban's Home and Go to Gilead (29:1–4)

29:1/ After Rachel had given birth to Joseph,[a] Laban went off to shear his sheep because they were a three-day journey removed from him. 2/ Jacob saw that Laban was going off to shear his sheep and summoned Leah and Rachel. He spoke tenderly with them so that they would come with him to the land of Canaan. 3/ For he told them how he had seen everything in a dream and everything about his statement to him that he should return to his father's house. They said, "We will go with you wherever you go." 4/ Jacob blessed the God of his father Isaac and the God of his grandfather Abraham. He set about loading up his wives and his children and took all his possessions. After he had crossed the river, he reached the land of Gilead. But Jacob had concealed his plan from Laban and had not told him.

The Encounter between Jacob and Laban in Gilead (29:5–8)

5/ During the seventh year of the fourth week [2135] Jacob returned to Gilead on the twenty-first day of the first month. Laban pursued him and found Jacob on the mountain of Gilead on the thirteenth (day) in the third month. 6/ But the Lord did not allow him to harm Jacob because he had appeared to him at night in a dream, and Laban told Jacob. 7/ On the fifteenth of those days Jacob prepared a banquet for Laban and all who had come with him. That day Jacob swore to Laban and Laban to Jacob that neither would commit an offense against the other on the mountain of Gilead with bad intentions. 8/ There he made a mound as a testimony: for

---

a At *Rachel had given birth to Joseph*, several Eth mss read *Leah had given birth to Issachar*.

this reason that place is named the mound of testimony after this mound.

A Digression on the Previous Name and Inhabitants of Gilead (29:9–11)

9/ But at first the land of Gilead was named the land of *Rafaem* because it was the land of the Rafaim. The Rafaim were born there,[a] giants whose heights were ten cubits, nine cubits, eight cubits, and (down) to seven cubits. 10/ The places where they lived (extended) from the land of the Ammonites as far as Mount Hermon. Their royal centers were Karnaim, Ashtaroth, Edrei, Misur, and Beon. 11/ The Lord destroyed them because of the evil things they did, for they were very wicked. The Amorites—evil and sinful—lived[b] in their place. Today there is no nation that has matched all their sins. They no longer have length of life on the earth.

Jacob Meets Esau and Cares for Isaac and Rebekah (29:12–20)

12/ Jacob sent Laban away, and he went to Mesopotamia, to the eastern country. But Jacob returned to the land of Gilead. 13/ He crossed the Jabbok on the eleventh of the ninth month, and on the same day his brother Esau came to him. They were reconciled with each other. Then he went from him to the land of Seir, while Jacob lived in tents. 14/ In the first year of the fifth week during this jubilee [2136] he crossed the Jordan. He settled on the other side of the Jordan and was tending his sheep from the sea of Fahahat[c] as far as Bethshan, Dothan, and the forest of Akrabbim. 15/ He sent his father Isaac some of all his possessions: clothing,

---

a The Eth mss lack *there*, while Lat has the word.

b Lat reads *caused/made live*, with *the Lord* as the assumed subject. Eth also reads a sing. third person verb which may preserve a remnant of the reading found in Lat.

c For interpreting this as a reference to the Sea of Galilee, see *Jubilees 22–50*, 809–10.

food, meat, things to drink, milk, butter, cheese, and some dates from the valley. 16/ To his mother Rebekah, too, (he sent goods) four times per year—between the seasons of the months, between plowing and harvest, between autumn and the rain(y season), and between winter and spring—to Abraham's tower. 17/ For Isaac had returned from the well of the oath, had gone up to the tower of his father Abraham, and had settled there away from his son Esau, 18/ because, at the time when Jacob went to Mesopotamia, Esau had married Mahalath, Ishmael's daughter. He had gathered all his father's flocks and his wives and had gone up and lived in Mount Seir. He had left his father Isaac alone at the well of the oath. 19/ So Isaac had gone up from the well of the oath and settled at the tower of his father Abraham in the mountain of Hebron. 20/ There Jacob would send everything that he was sending to his father and mother from time to time—everything they needed.[a] Then they would bless Jacob with all their mind and with all their being.

Dinah, Shechem, Exogamy, and Levi the Priest (Chapter 30)

The Story about the Rape of Dinah and the Response by Jacob and His Sons (30:1–4)

30:1/ During the first year of the sixth week [2143] he went up safely to Salem, which is on the east side of Shechem, in the fourth month. 2/ There Jacob's daughter Dinah was taken by force to the house of Shechem, the son of Hamor the Hivite, the ruler of the land. He lay with her and defiled her. Now she was a small girl, twelve years of age. 3/ He begged her father[b] and her brothers that she become his wife. Jacob and his sons were angry with the Shechemites because they had defiled their sister Dinah. They spoke deceptively with them, acted in a crafty way toward them, and deceived them.[c] 4/ Simeon

---

a Lat adds *in their every want.*

b Many Eth copies add *that she be given to him as a wife.* Lat does not have these words.

c For the last two clauses Lat reads *Simeon and Levi mocked them in a crafty way.*

and Levi entered Shechem unexpectedly[a] and effected a punishment on all the Shechemites. They killed every man whom they found in it. They left absolutely no one in it. They killed everyone in a painful way because they had violated their sister Dinah.

There Is to Be No Such Defilement in Israel (30:5–10)

5/ Nothing like this is to be done anymore from now on—to defile an Israelite woman. For the punishment had been decreed against them in heaven that they were to annihilate all the Shechemites with the sword, since they had done something shameful in Israel. 6/ The Lord handed them over to Jacob's sons for them to uproot them with the sword and to effect punishment against them and so that there should not again be something like this within Israel—defiling an Israelite virgin. 7/ If there is a man in Israel who wishes to give his daughter or his sister to any foreigner, he is to die. He is to be stoned because he has done something shameful within Israel. The woman is to be burned because she has defiled the reputation of her father's house; she is to be uprooted from Israel. 8/ No prostitute or impurity is to be found within Israel throughout all the time of the earth's history, for Israel is holy to the Lord. Any man who has defiled it is to die; he is to be stoned. 9/ For this is the way it has been ordained and written on the heavenly tablets regarding any descendant of Israel who defiles (it): "He is to die; he is to be stoned." 10/ This law has no temporal end. There is no remission or any forgiveness; but rather the man who has defiled his daughter within all of Israel is to be eradicated because he has given one of his descendants to Molech[b] and has sinned by defiling it.

No Marriage with Non-Israelites (30:11–16)

11/ Now you, Moses, order the Israelites and testify to them that they are not to give any of their daughters to foreigners

---

a For this clause Lat has *Simeon and Levi resolved to destroy them.*

b Lat reads *to a foreigner*, which is an interpretation of *to Molech* (Lev 18:21; 20:2).

and that they are not to marry any foreign women because it is despicable before the Lord. 12/ For this reason I have written for you in the words of the law everything that the Shechemites did to Dinah and how Jacob's sons said: "We will not give our daughter to a man who has a foreskin because for us that would be a disgraceful thing." 13/ It is a disgraceful thing for the Israelites who give or take (in marriage) one of the foreign women because it is too impure and despicable for Israel. 14/ Israel will not become clean from this impurity while it has one of the foreign women or if anyone has given one of his daughters to any foreign man.[a] 15/ For it is blow upon blow and curse upon curse. Every punishment, blow, and curse will come. If one does this or shuts his eyes to those who do impure things and who defile the Lord's sanctuary and to those who profane his holy name, then the entire nation will be condemned together because of all this impurity and this contamination. 16/ There will be no favoritism or partiality; there will be no receiving from him of fruit, sacrifices, offerings, fat, or the aroma of a pleasing fragrance so that he should accept it. (So) is any man or woman in Israel to be who defiles his sanctuary.

The Example of Simeon and Levi (30:17–23)

17/ For this reason I have ordered you: "Proclaim this testimony to Israel: 'See how it turned out for the Shechemites and their children—how they were handed over to Jacob's two sons. They killed them in a painful way. It was a just act for them and was recorded as a just act for them.' 18/ Levi's descendants were chosen for the priesthood and as Levites to serve before the Lord as we (do) for all time. Levi and his sons will be blessed forever because he was eager to carry out justice, punishment, and revenge on all who rise[b] against Israel. 19/ So blessing and justice before the God of all are entered

---

a At the words *or—man* Lat reads *and we will not become clean (from?) one of our daughters.* See *Jubilees 22–50*, 816.

b Lat has *were placed.*

for him as a testimony on the heavenly tablets. 20/ We ourselves remember the justice which the man performed during his lifetime at all times of the year. As far as 1,000 generations will they enter (it). It will come to him and his family[a] after him. He has been recorded on the heavenly tablets as a friend and a just man."

21/ I have written this entire message for you and have ordered you to tell the Israelites not to sin or transgress the statutes or violate the covenant that was established for them so that they should perform it and be recorded as friends. 22/ But if they transgress and behave in any impure ways, they will be recorded on the heavenly tablets as enemies. They will be erased from the book of the living and will be recorded in the book of those who will be destroyed and with those who will be uprooted from the earth. 23/ On the day that Jacob's sons killed (the people of) Shechem, a written notice was entered in heaven for them (to the effect) that they had carried out what was right, justice, and revenge against the sinners. It was[b] recorded as a blessing.

The End of the Episode (30:24–26)

24/ They led their sister Dinah from Shechem's house and captured everything that was in Shechem—their sheep, cattle, and donkeys; all their property and all their flocks—and brought everything to their father Jacob. 25/ He spoke with them about the fact that they had killed[c] (the people of) a city because he was afraid of the people who were living in the land—of the Canaanites and the Perizzites. 26/ A fear of the Lord was in all the cities which were around Shechem. They did not set out to pursue Jacob's sons because terror had fallen on them.

---

 a Eth could be translated *generations* (Deut 7:9); Lat reads *seed/descendants*.
 b A strongly supported reading among the Eth mss and in Lat is *They were*.
 c Lat *destroyed*.

Bethel (1). Jacob Sees His Parents and Isaac Blesses Levi and Judah (Chapter 31)

Preparations and Travel to Bethel (31:1–3a)

31:1/ On the first of the month Jacob told all the people of his household: "Purify yourselves and change your clothes; we are to set out and go up to Bethel where I made a vow, on the day that I ran away from my brother Esau, to the one who has been with me and has brought me back safely to this land. Remove the foreign gods that are among you." 2/ They *handed over*[a] the foreign gods, their earrings and their necklaces, and the idols that Rachel had stolen from her father Laban. She gave everything to Jacob, and he burned them, broke them into pieces, demolished them, and hid them beneath the oak that is in the land of Shechem. 3a/ On the first of the seventh month he went up to Bethel. He built an altar at the place where he had slept and had set up a pillar.

Jacob, His Parents, and His Two Sons Levi and Judah (31:3b–30a)

Invitations, Arrival with Levi and Judah, and Meeting with Rebekah (31:3b–7)

3b/ He sent word to his father Isaac and to his mother Rebekah as well to come to him to his sacrifice. 4/ Isaac said, "Let my son Jacob come so that I can see him before I die." 5/ Jacob went to his father Isaac and his mother Rebekah in the house of his father Abraham. He took two of his sons with him—Levi and Judah. He came to his father Isaac and his mother Rebekah. 6/ Rebekah went out of the tower into the tower gates to kiss Jacob and hug him because she had revived at the time she heard (the report): "Your son Jacob has now arrived." She kissed him. 7/ When she saw his two sons, she recognized them. She said to him, "Are these your sons, my

---

a The Eth reading *melted* seems inappropriate in the context. It may be that a confusion between two look-alike verbs in Heb or Eth led to the reading (*Jubilees 22–50*, 845).

son?" She hugged them, kissed them, and blessed them as follows: "Through you Abraham's descendants will become famous. You will become a blessing on the earth."

Meeting with Isaac and Blessing of Levi and Judah (31:8–20)

Introduction to the Scene (31:8–12)

8/ Jacob went in to his father Isaac, to his bedroom where he was lying down. His two children were with him. He took his father's hand, bent down, and kissed him. Isaac hung on his son Jacob's neck and cried on his neck. 9/ Then the shadow passed from Isaac's eyes and he saw Jacob's two sons—Levi and Judah—and said, "Are these your sons, my son, because they look like you?" 10/ He told him that they were indeed his sons:[a] "You have noticed correctly, father,[b] that they are my sons." 11/ When they came up to him, he turned to them and hugged both[c] of them together. 12/ A spirit of prophecy descended into his mouth. He took Levi by his right hand and Judah by his left hand.

Isaac's Blessing of Levi (31:13–17)

13/ He turned to Levi first and began to bless him first.
He said to him, "May the Lord of everything—he is the
   Lord of all ages—bless you and your sons throughout
   all ages.
14/ May the Lord give you and your descendants greatness
   and honor;[d]
may he make you and your descendants (alone) out of all
   humanity approach him
to serve in his temple like the angels of the presence and
   like the holy ones.
The descendants of your sons will be like them in honor,
   greatness, and holiness.

---

a Lat makes the statement a direct address: *they are indeed my sons.*

b Lat has the correct reading; Eth strangely repeats the word *truly/indeed.*

c So Lat; Eth has *all.*

d Greatness and *honor* are mentioned, though in slightly different expressions, in Eth and Lat (*Jubilees 22–50*, 845).

May he make them great throughout all the ages.
15/ They will be princes, judges, and leaders of all the
    descendants of Jacob's sons.
They will declare the word of the Lord justly
and will justly judge all his verdicts.
They will tell my ways to Jacob
and my paths to Israel.
The blessing of the Lord will be placed in their mouth,[a]
so that they may bless all the descendants of the beloved.
16/ Your mother named you Levi,
and she has given you the right name.
You will become one who is joined to[b] the Lord
and a companion of all Jacob's sons.
His table is to belong to you;
you and your sons are to eat (from) it.
May your table be filled throughout all history;
may your food not be lacking throughout all ages.
17/ May all who hate you fall before you,
and all your enemies be uprooted and perish.
May the one who blesses you be blessed,
and any nation who curses you be cursed."

Isaac's Blessing of Judah (31:18–20)
18/   Then he said to Judah:
"May the Lord give you the power and strength to trample
    on all who hate you.
Be a prince—you and one of your sons—for Jacob's sons.
May your name and the name of your sons be one
that goes and travels around[c] in the entire earth and the
    regions.
Then the nations will be frightened before you;
all the nations will be disturbed;
all peoples will be disturbed.

---

  a Lat reads *to his seed*.

  b Lat *for the adornment of* probably arose from a misreading of the Heb etymology of *Levi* (*Jubilees 22–50*, 846).

  c Lat *possess* may have resulted from confusing two Greek verbs.

19/ May Jacob's help be in you;
May Israel's safety be found in you.
20/ At the time when you sit on the honorable throne that is rightly yours,
there will be great peace for all the descendants of the beloved's sons.
The one who blesses you will be blessed,
and all who hate and trouble you,
and those, too, who curse you
will be uprooted and destroyed from the earth
and are to be cursed."

Further Conversation with Isaac (31:21–30a)

21/ He turned, kissed him again, and hugged him. He was very happy that he had seen the sons of his true son Jacob. 22/ He moved out from between his feet, fell down, and bowed to him. He then blessed them. He rested there near his father Isaac that night. They ate and drank happily. 23/ He made Jacob's two sons sleep, one on his right, and one on his left; and it was credited to him as something righteous.

24/ That night Jacob told his father everything—how the Lord had shown him great kindness, that he had directed all his ways favorably and had protected him from evil. 25/ Isaac blessed the God of his father Abraham who had not put an end to his mercy and faithfulness for the son of his servant Isaac. 26/ In the morning Jacob told his father Isaac the vow that he had made to the Lord, the vision that he had seen, that he had built an altar and everything was ready for offering the sacrifice before the Lord as he had vowed, and that he had come to put him on a donkey. 27/ But Isaac said to his son Jacob, "I am unable to come with you because I am old and unable to put up with the trip. Go safely, my son, because I am 165 years of age today. I am no longer able to travel. Put your mother on an animal and let her go with you. 28/ I know, my son, that it was on my account that you came. Blessed be this day on which you have seen me alive and I, too, have seen you, my son. 29/ Be successful and carry out the vow that you made.

Do not delay (in carrying out) your vow because you will be held accountable regarding the vow. Now hurry to perform it. May the one who has made everything, to whom you made the vow, be pleased (with it)." 30a/ He said to Rebekah, "Go with your son Jacob."

Return to Bethel and Joyful Reflection on His Father's Blessings (31:30b–32)

30b/ So Rebekah went with her son Jacob and Deborah with her. They arrived at Bethel. 31/ When Jacob recalled the prayer with which his father had blessed him and his two sons—Levi and Judah—he was very happy and blessed the God of his fathers Abraham and Isaac. 32/ He said, "Now I know that I and my sons, too, have an eternal hope before the God of all." This is the way it is ordained regarding the two of them, and it is entered for them as an eternal testimony on the heavenly tablets just as Isaac blessed them.

Bethel (2): Tithing, Temple-Building, and Departure (Chapter 32)

Bethel (32:1–29)

Levi's Dream (32:1)

32:1/ That night he stayed at Bethel. Levi dreamed that he—he and his sons[a]—was appointed and ordained to the priesthood of the Most High God forever. When he awakened, he blessed the Lord.

Jacob's Tithes (32:2–9)

2/ Jacob got up early in the morning on the fourteenth day of this month and gave a tithe of all that had come with him—from people to animals, from money to all utensils and clothing. He gave a tithe of all. 3/ At that time Rachel

---

a Lat lacks *he and his sons*.

was pregnant with her son Benjamin. Jacob counted his sons from him. He went up (the list), and it came down on Levi in the Lord's share. His father put priestly clothes on him and ordained him. 4/ On the fifteenth of this month he brought to the altar 14 young bulls from the cattle, 28 rams, 49 sheep, 7[a] kids, and 21[b] goats—as a burnt offering on the altar and as a pleasing offering for a pleasant aroma before God. 5/ This was his gift because of the vow which he had made that he would give a tithe along with their sacrifices and their libations. 6/ When the fire had consumed it, he would burn incense on the fire above it; and as a peace offering two young bulls, four rams, four sheep, four he-goats, two year-old sheep, and two goats. This is what he would do daily for the seven days. 7/ He was eating happily there—he, all his sons, and his men—for the seven days. He was blessing and praising the Lord who had freed him from all his difficulties and who had granted him his vow. 8/ He tithed all the clean animals and made an offering of them. He gave his son Levi the unclean animals and gave him all the persons of the people. 9/ Levi rather than his ten brothers served as priest in Bethel before his father Jacob. There he was a priest, and Jacob gave what he had vowed. In this way he again gave a tithe to the Lord. He sanctified it, and it became holy.

Tithes (32:10–15)

10/ For this reason it is ordained as a law on the heavenly tablets to tithe a second time, to eat it before the Lord—year by year—in the place that has been chosen (as the site) where his name will reside. This law has no temporal limits forever. 11/ That statute has been written down so that it should be carried out year by year—to eat the tithe a second time before the Lord in the place that has been chosen. One is not to leave any of it over from this year to the next year. 12/ For the seed is to be

---

a Due to a mistaken reading of a Greek number, Eth reads *60*.
b Also due to misreading a Greek number, Eth has *29*.

eaten in its year until the time for harvesting the seed of the year; the wine (will be drunk) until the time for wine; and the olive (will be used) until the proper time of its season. 13/ Any of it that is left over and grows old is to be (considered) contaminated; it is to be burned up because it has become impure. 14/ In this way they are to eat it at the same time[a] in the sanctuary; they are not to let it grow old. 15/ The entire tithe of cattle and sheep is holy to the Lord, and is to belong to his priests who will eat (it) before him year by year, because this is the way it is ordained and inscribed on the heavenly tablets regarding the tithe.

Night Appearances to Jacob (32:16–26)

16/ During the next night, on the twenty-second day of this month, Jacob decided to build up that place and to surround the courtyard with a wall, to sanctify it, and make it eternally holy for himself and for his children after him forever. 17/ The Lord appeared to him during the night. He blessed him and said to him, "You are not to be called Jacob only but you will (also) be named Israel." 18/ He said to him a second time, "I am the Lord who created heaven and earth. I will increase your numbers and multiply you very much. Kings will come from you, and they will rule wherever humanity has set foot. 19/ I will give your descendants all of the land[b] that is beneath the sky. They will rule over all the nations just as they wish. Afterwards, they will gain the entire earth, and they will possess it forever." 20/ When he had finished speaking with him, he went up from him, and Jacob kept watching until he had gone up into heaven. 21/ In a night vision he saw an angel coming down from heaven with seven tablets in his hands. He gave (them) to Jacob, and he read them. He learned everything that was written in them—what would happen to him and his sons throughout all ages. 22/ After he had shown him

---

a The expression *at the same time* could be rendered *together*.
b Lat has *blessings*.

everything that was written on the tablets, he said to him, "Do not build up this place, and do not make it an eternal temple. Do not live here because this is not the place. Go to the house[a] of your father Abraham and live where your father Isaac is until the day of your father's death. 23/ For you will die peacefully in Egypt and be buried honorably in this land in the grave of your fathers—with Abraham and Isaac. 24/ Do not be afraid because everything will happen just as you have seen and read. Now you write down everything just as you have seen and read." 25/ Then Jacob said, "Lord, how shall I remember everything just as I have read and seen?" He said to him, "I will remind you of everything." 26/ When he had gone from him, he awakened and remembered everything that he had read and seen. He wrote down all the things that he had read and seen.

An Extra Day (32:27–29)

27/ He celebrated one more day there. On it he sacrificed exactly as he had been sacrificing on the previous days. He named it Detaining because he was detained[b] one day. He named the previous ones the Festival. 28/ This is the way it was revealed that it should be, and it is written on the heavenly tablets. For this reason it was revealed to him that he should celebrate it and add it to the seven days of the festival. 29/ It was called Detaining because of the fact that it is entered[c] in the testimony of the festal days in accord with the number of days in the year.

Departure from Bethel (32:30–34)

30/ In the night, on the twenty-third of this month, Deborah, Rebekah's nurse, died. They buried her below the city,

---

a Lat reads *the place, the tower.*

b At *Detaining ... detained* Eth reads *Addition ... added* (also in v 29; see *Jubilees 22–50*, 869).

c Lat has *it is added.*

beneath the oak (near) the stream. He named that place the Stream of Deborah and the oak the Oak of Mourning for Deborah.

31/ Then Rebecca set out and returned home to his father Isaac. Through her Jacob sent rams, he-goats, and sheep to make his father a meal as he would wish. 32/ He followed his mother until he reached the country of Kabratan, and he remained there. 33/ During the night Rachel gave birth to a son. She named him Son of my Pain because she had difficulty when she was giving birth to him. But his father named him Benjamin on the eleventh of the eighth month, during the first year of the sixth week of this jubilee [2143]. 34/ Rachel died there and was buried in the country of Ephrathah, that is, Bethlehem. Jacob built a pillar at Rachel's grave—on the road above her grave.

Reuben's Sin with Bilhah and Jacob's Move to the House of Abraham (Chapter 33)

Jacob and Leah's Absence and Reuben's Sin with Bilhah (33:1–9a)

33:1/ Jacob went and stayed to the south of the tower of Eder Ephrathah. He went to his father Isaac—he and his wife Leah—on the first of the tenth month. 2/ When Reuben saw Bilhah, Rachel's maid—his father's concubine—bathing in water in a hidden place, he loved her. 3/ He entered Bilhah's house secretly at night[a] and found her lying alone in her bed and sleeping in her tent. 4/ After he had slept with her, she awakened and saw that Reuben was lying with her in bed. She uncovered the edge of her (clothing), took hold of him, shouted out, and realized that it was Reuben. 5/ She was ashamed because of him.[b] Once she had released her grip on him, he[c] ran away. 6/ She grieved terribly about this mat-

---

a The first words of the verse follow the readings of Lat Syr; Eth has *At night he hid. He entered Bilhah's house at night* (*Jubilees 22–50*, 899).

b For this first sentence of the verse Lat reads *He was confused by her*.

c A few Eth mss read *she*; the gender of the pronoun in Lat is ambiguous.

ter and told no one at all. 7/ When Jacob came and looked for her, she said to him, "I am not pure for you because I am contaminated from you, since Reuben defiled me and slept with me at night. I was sleeping and did not realize (it) until he uncovered the edge of my (garment) and lay with me." 8/ Jacob was very angry at Reuben because he had lain with Bilhah, since he had uncovered the covering of his father. 9a/ Jacob did not know[a] her again because Reuben had defiled her.

The Angel's Address to Moses (33:9b–20)

The Law regarding the Sin (33:9b–12)

9b/ As for any man who uncovers the covering of his father—his act is indeed very bad and it is indeed despicable before the Lord. 10/ For this reason it is written and ordained on the heavenly tablets that a man is not to sleep with his father's wife and that he is not to uncover the covering of his father because it is impure. They are certainly to die together—the man who sleeps with his father's wife and the woman, too—because they have done something impure on the earth. 11/ There is to be nothing impure before our God within the nation that he has chosen as his own possession. 12/ Again, it is written a second time: "Let the one who sleeps with his father's wife be cursed because he has uncovered his father's covering.[b] All of the Lord's holy ones said, 'So be it, so be it.'"

Commands for Israel and the Special Case of Reuben (33:13–17)

13/ Now you order the Israelites to observe this command because it is a capital offense and it is an impure thing. To eternity there is no expiation to atone for the man who does this;[c]

---

a So Lat Syr; Eth reads *approach*.
b So 4Q221 4 2; Eth has *shame*.
c 4Q221 4 5, which has more space than implied by the Eth wording, may have read *this evil thing* (DJD 13:73, 75).

but he is <u>to be put to death, to be ston</u>ed, and to be killed and uprooted from among the people of our God. 14/ Fo<u>r</u> any man wh<u>o commits it in Israel</u> <u>will not be allowed to live</u> a single <u>day</u> on the earth because he is despicable and impure. 15/ <u>They are</u> not to <u>say,</u> "<u>Reuben was allowed</u> to live and (have) forgiveness after he had slept with the concub<u>ine</u>[a] <u>of his father</u> while she had a husband and her husband—his father Jacob—was alive." 16/ For the statute, the punishment, and the law had not been completely revealed to all but (only) in your time as a law of its particular time and as an eternal law for the history of eternity. 17/ There is no time when this law will be at an end, nor is there any forgiveness for it; rather both of them are to be uprooted among the people. On the day in which they have done this they are to kill them.

Israel as a Holy Nation (33:18–20)

18/ Now you, Moses, write for Israel so that they keep it and do not act like this and do not stray into a capital offense; because the Lord our God, who shows no favoritism and takes no bribe, is the judge. 19/ Tell them these words of the covenant so that they may listen, guard themselves, be careful about them, and not be destroyed or uprooted from the earth. For all who commit it on the earth before the Lord are impure, something detestable, a blemish and something contaminated. 20/ No sin is greater than the sexual impurity that they commit on the earth because Israel is a holy people for the Lord its God. It is the nation that he possesses; it is a priestly nation; it is a priestly kingdom; it is what he owns.[b] No such impurity will be seen among the holy people.

---

a 4Q221 4 10 seems to have the last letter of *concubine*; Eth has *concubine wife*.
b For the last two clauses in the verse, see *Jubilees 22–50*, 901.

Jacob and His Family Move to the House of Abraham (33:21–23)

21/ During the third year of the sixth week [2145] Jacob and all his sons went and took up residence at the house of Abraham near his father Isaac and his mother Rebekah. 22/ These are the names of Jacob's sons: Reuben, his firstborn, Simeon, Levi, Judah, Issachar, Zebulun were Leah's sons. Rachel's sons were Joseph and Benjamin. Bilhah's sons were Dan and Naphtali. And Zilpah's sons were Gad and Asher. Leah's daughter Dinah was Jacob's only daughter. 23/ After they had come, they bowed to Isaac and Rebekah. When they saw them, they blessed Jacob and all his children. Isaac was extremely happy that he had seen the children of his younger son Jacob, and he blessed them.

War with the Amorite Kings, Joseph and His Brothers, the Day of Atonement, and the Wives of Jacob's Sons (Chapter 34)

War with Seven Amorite Kings (34:1–9)

34:1/ During the sixth year of this week of this forty-fourth jubilee [2148], Jacob sent his sons to tend his sheep—his servants were also with them—to the field of Shechem. 2/ Seven Amorite kings assembled against them to kill them from their hiding place beneath the trees[a] and to take their animals as booty. 3/ But Jacob, Levi, Judah, and Joseph remained at home with their father Isaac because he was distressed and they were unable to leave him. Benjamin was the youngest, and for this reason he stayed with him. 4/ Then came the kings of Tafu, the king of Ares, the king of Seragan, the king of Selo, the king of Gaaz, the king of Betoron, the king of Maanisakir, and all who were living on this mountain, who[b]

---

[a] In place of *to kill them from their hiding place beneath the trees*, Lat reads *and waited in the woods in order that they might kill them*.

[b] Lat and a few Eth copies place *and* before *who*, so that the relative pronoun introduces a second group.

were living in the forest in the land of Canaan. 5/ It was reported to Jacob: "The Amorite kings have just surrounded your sons and have carried off your flocks by force." 6/ He set out from his house—he, his three sons, all his father's servants, and his servants—and went against them with 6,000 men who carried swords. 7/ He killed them in the field of Shechem, and they pursued the ones who ran away. He killed them with the blade of the sword. He killed Ares, Tafu, Saregan, Silo, Amanisakir, and Gagaas 8/ and collected his flocks. He got control of them and imposed tribute on them so that they should give him as tribute one-fifth of their land's products. He built Robel and Tamnatares 9/ and returned safely. He made peace with them, and they became his servants until the day that he and his sons went down to Egypt.

Joseph and His Brothers (34:10–19)

Joseph's Mission to His Brothers (34:10)

10/ During the seventh year of this week [2149] he sent Joseph from his house to the land of Shechem to find out about his brothers' welfare. He found them in the land of Dothan.

Their Harsh Treatment of Joseph (34:11)

11/ They acted in a treacherous way and made a plan against him to kill him; but, after changing their minds, they sold him to a traveling band of Ishmaelites. They brought him down to Egypt and sold him to Potiphar, Pharaoh's eunuch, the chief cook, and the priest of the city of Elew.

Jacob's Grief and the Day of Atonement (34:12–19)

12/ Jacob's son's slaughtered a he-goat, stained Joseph's clothing by dipping it in its blood, and sent (it) to their father Jacob on the tenth of the seventh month. 13/ He mourned all that night[a] because they had brought it to him in the evening.

---

a Many Eth mss read *day*.

He became feverish through mourning his death and said that a wild animal had eaten Joseph. That day all the people of his household mourned with him. They continued to be distressed and to mourn with him all that day. 14/ His sons and daughter set about consoling him, but he was inconsolable for his son. 15/ That day Bilhah heard that Joseph had perished. While she was mourning for him, she died. She had been living in Qafratefa. His daughter Dinah, too, died after Joseph had perished. These three (reasons for) mourning came to Israel in one month. 16/ They buried Bilhah opposite Rachel's grave, and they buried his daughter Dinah there as well. 17/ He continued mourning for Joseph for one year and was not comforted but said, "May I go down to the grave mourning for my son." 18/ For this reason, it has been ordained regarding the Israelites that they should be distressed on the tenth of the seventh month—on the day when (the news) that made (him) lament Joseph reached his father Jacob—in order to make atonement for themselves on it with a kid—on the tenth of the seventh month, once a year—for their sins. For they had saddened their father's (feelings of) affection for his son Joseph. 19/ This day has been ordained so that they may be saddened on it for their sins, all their transgressions, and all their errors; so that they may purify themselves on this day once a year.

The Wives of Jacob's Sons (34:20-21)

20/ After Joseph had perished, Jacob's sons took wives for themselves. The name of Reuben's wife was Oda; the name of Simeon's wife was Adebaa, the Canaanitess; the name of Levi's wife was Melcha, one of the daughters of Aram—one of the descendants of Terah's sons; the name of Judah's wife was Betasuel, the Canaanitess; the name of Issachar's wife was Hezaqa; the name of Zebulun's wife was [Neeman];[a] the

---

a The older Eth mss lack a name; a few copies present something like the name in brackets. A Syr list of the names of the patriarchs' wives in Jubilees names her *'dny*.

name of Dan's wife was Egla; the name of Naphtali's wife was Rasu'u of Mesopotamia; the name of Gad's wife was Maka; the name of Asher's wife was Iyona; the name of Joseph's wife was Asenath, the Egyptian, and the name of Benjamin's wife was Iyaska. 21/ Simeon, after changing his mind, married another woman from Mesopotamia like his brothers.

The Last Instructions and Death of Rebekah (Chapter 35)

Conversation between Rebekah and Jacob (35:1–8)

35:1/ During the first year of the first week in the forty-fifth jubilee [2157], Rebekah summoned her son Jacob and ordered him regarding his father and brother that he was to honor them throughout Jacob's entire lifetime. 2/ Jacob said, "I will do everything just as you ordered me because this matter will be something honorable and great for me; it will be a righteous act for me before the Lord that I should honor them. 3/ You, mother, know everything I have done and all my thoughts from the day I was born until today—that at all times I think of doing good for all. 4/ How shall I not do what you have ordered me—that I should honor my father and brother? 5/ Tell me,[a] mother, what impropriety you have noticed in me and I will certainly turn away from it and will experience mercy." 6/ She said to him, "My son, throughout my entire lifetime I have noticed no improper act in you but only proper one(s). However, I will tell you the truth, my son: I will die during this year and will not make it alive through this year because I have seen the day of my death in a dream[b]—that I will not live more than 155[c] years. Now I have completed my entire lifetime that I am to live." 7/ Jacob laughed at what his mother was saying because his mother said to him that she would die, but she was sitting in front of him in possession of her strength. She had lost none of her

---

a Lat *I ask. Tell me* could be original (*Jubilees 22–50*, 937).
b Lat lacks most of the clause from *because* to *dream*, reading only *I will die*.
c Lat may lack the *five* in *155* (*Jubilees 22–50*, 938).

strength because she could come and go; she could see and her teeth were strong. No sickness had touched her throughout her entire lifetime. 8/ Jacob said to her, "Mother, I would be fortunate if my lifetime approached your lifetime and (if) my strength would remain with me in the way your strength has. You are not going to die but rather have jokingly spoken idle nonsense with me about your death."

Conversation between Rebekah and Isaac (35:9–17)

9/ She went in to Isaac and said to him, "I am making one request of you: make Esau swear that he will not harm Jacob and not pursue him in hatred. For you know the inclination of Esau—that he has been malicious since his youth and that he is devoid of virtue because he wishes to kill him after your death.[a] 10/ You know everything that he has done[b] from the day his brother Jacob went to Haran until today—that he has wholeheartedly abandoned us. He has treated us badly; he has led away your flocks and has taken all your possessions away from you by force. 11/ When we would ask him in a pleading way for what belongs to us, he would again do something treacherous[c] like someone who was being charitable to us. 12/ He is embittered toward you due to the fact that you blessed your perfect and true son Jacob since he has virtue only, no evil. From the time he came from Haran until today he has not deprived us of anything but he always brings us everything in its season. He is wholeheartedly happy when we accept (anything) from him, and he blesses us. He has not separated from us from the day he came from Haran until today. He has continually been living with us at home (all the while) honoring us." 13/ Isaac said to her, "I, too, know and see the actions of Jacob who

---

a The words from *and that he is devoid* through *death* are confirmed by 4Q223–224 2 i:49 where the text survives, but 1Q18 lacks them.

b 4Q223–224 2 i:50 adds *with/to us*, but 1Q18, Eth, and Lat lack the prepositional phrase.

c The reading follows 4Q223–224 2 i:52; Eth has only *would do/act*.

is with us—that he wholeheartedly honors us and does our wishes.[a] At first I did love Esau much more than Jacob, after he was born; but now I love Jacob more than Esau because he has done so many bad things and lacks (the ability to do) what is right. For the entire way he acts is (characterized by) violence and wickedness and there is no justice about him. 14/ Now my mind is disturbed about his actions. Neither he nor his descendants are to be saved because they will be destroyed from the earth and uprooted from beneath the sky. For he has abandoned the God of Abraham and has gone after the impurity of the women and after the error of the women.[b] 15/ You are saying to me that I should make him swear not to kill his brother Jacob. If he does swear, he will not persevere[c] and will not do what is virtuous but rather what is evil. 16/ If he wishes to kill his brother Jacob, he will be handed over to Jacob and will not escape from his control but will fall into his control. 17/ Now you are not to be afraid for Jacob because Jacob's guardian is greater and more powerful, glorious, and praiseworthy than Esau's guardian. For like dust befor[e   ] all the guardians of Esau before the God of [J]acob [my perfect and de]ar s[on.] But I lo[ve   do]es our wishes [   ] my sister in peace."[d]

Conversation between Rebekah and Esau (35:18–24)

18/ Then Rebekah sent and summoned Esau. When he had come to her, she said to him: "I have a request that I will make of you, my son; say that you will do it, my son." 19/ He said, "I

---

a 4Q223–224 2 ii:4; Eth lacks *and does our wishes*.

b The reading follows 4Q223–224 2 ii:8; Eth has *after his wives, after impurity, and after their errors—he and his sons*.

c So 4Q223–224 2 ii:9; Eth *be*.

d After *Esau's guardian* in v 17 and the beginning of v 18 4Q223–224 2 ii has two lines of text that are lacking in Eth. The legible letters on the lines indicate that their content resembled the scene in Jub 27:13–17.

will do anything you tell me; I will not refuse your request." 20/ She said to him: "I ask of you that on the day I die you bring me and bury me near your father's mother Sarah; and that you and Jacob love one another, and that the one not desire harm for his brother but only love for one another. Then you will be prosperous, my sons, and be honored on the earth. Your enemy will not be happy over you. You will become a blessing and an object of kindness in the view of all who love you." 21/ He said, "I will do everything that you say to me. I will bury you on the day of your death near my father's mother Sarah as you have desired that her bones be near your bones. 22/ My brother Jacob I will love more than all humanity. I have no brother on the entire earth but him alone. This is no great thing for me if I love him because he is my brother. We were conceived together in your belly and we emerged together from your *womb*.[a] If I do not love my brother, whom shall I love? 23/ I myself ask of you that you instruct Jacob about me and my sons because I know that he will indeed rule over me and my sons. For on the day when my father blessed him he made him the superior and me the inferior one. 24/ I swear to you that I will love him and that throughout my entire lifetime I will not desire harm for him but only what is good." He swore to her about this entire matter.

Esau and Jacob with Rebekah (35:25–26)

25/ She summoned Jacob in front of Esau and gave him orders in line with what she had discussed with Esau. 26/ He said, "I will do what pleases you. Trust me that nothing bad against Esau will come from me or my sons. I will not be first except in love only."

---

[a] The Eth reading with the strongest support in the mss is *mercy*. The reading resulted when two similar Heb words were confused (*Jubilees 22–50*, 940).

Esau and Jacob's Final Meal with Rebekah and Her Death (35:27)

27/ She and her sons ate and drank that night. She died that night at the age of three jubilees, one week, and one year [= 155 years]. Her two sons Esau and Jacob buried her in the twofold cave near their father's mother Sarah.

Isaac's Last Day and the Death of Leah (Chapter 36)

Isaac's Instructions regarding His Burial and His Testament to Esau and Jacob (36:1–11)

36:1/ During the sixth year of this week [2162] Isaac summoned his two sons Esau and Jacob. When they had come to him, he said to them: "My children, I am going the way of my fathers, to the eternal home where my fathers are. 2/ Bury me near my father Abraham in the double cave in the field of Ephron the Hittite that Abraham acquired to (have) a burial place there. There, in the grave that I dug for myself, bury me. 3/ This is what I am ordering you, my sons: that you do what is right and just on the earth so that the Lord may bring on you everything that the Lord said that he would do for Abraham and his descendants. 4/ Practice brotherly love among yourselves, my sons, like a man who loves himself, with each one desiring what is good for his brother and doing things together[a] on the earth. May they love one another as themselves. 5/ Regarding the matter of idols, I am instructing[b] you to reject them, to be an enemy of them, and not to love them because they are full of errors for those who worship them and who bow to them. 6/ My sons, remember the Lord, the God of your father Abraham—afterwards I, too, worshiped and served him properly and sincerely—so that he may make you numerous and increase your descendants in number like the stars of the sky and plant you in the earth as a righteous plant that will not be uprooted throughout all

---

a Many Eth mss add *from the heart*.
b Many Eth copies have *commanding*.

the history of eternity. 7/ Now I will make you swear with the great oath—because there is no oath which is greater than it, by the praiseworthy, glorious, and great, splendid, marvelous, powerful, and great name which made the heavens and the earth and everything together—that you will continue to fear and worship him, 8/ as each loves his brother kindly and properly. One is not to desire harm for his brother from now and forever, throughout your entire lifetime, so that you may be prosperous in everything that you do and not be destroyed. 9/ If one of you desires harm for his brother, be aware from now on that anyone who desires harm for his fellow[a] will fall into his control and will be uprooted from the land of the living, while his descendants will be destroyed from beneath the sky. 10/ On the day of anger with raging wrath and fury[b]—with a blazing fire that devours—he will burn his land, his cities, and everything that belongs to him just as he burned Sodom. He will be erased from the disciplinary book of humanity. He will not be entered in the book of life but is one who[c] will be destroyed. He will pass over to an eternal curse so that their punishment may always be renewed with denunciation and curse, with anger, pain, and wrath, and with blows and eternal sickness. 11/ I am reporting and testifying to you, my sons, in accord with the punishment that will come on the man who wishes to do what is harmful to his brother."

Isaac Divides His Estate, Dies, and Is Buried (36:12–18)

12/ That day he divided all the property that he owned between the two of them. He gave the larger part to the man who was the first to be born along with the tower, everything around it, and everything that Abraham had acquired at the well of the oath. 13/ He said, "I am making this portion larger for

---

a So 4Q223–224 2 ii:51; almost all Eth mss read *for his brother.*

b The reading with three nouns follows 4Q223–224 2 ii:52; the best Eth reading offers four similar nouns.

c Many Eth copies have *in the one that.*

the man who was the first to be born." 14/ But Esau said, "I sold (it) to Jacob; I gave my birthright to Jacob. It is to be given to him. I will say absolutely nothing about it because it belongs to him." 15/ Isaac then said, "May a blessing rest on you, my sons, and on your descendants today because you have given me rest. My mind is not sad regarding the birthright—lest you do something evil about it. 16/ May the Most High Lord bless the man who does what is right—him and his descendants forever." 17/ When he had finished giving them orders and blessing them, they ate and drank together in front of him. He was happy because there was agreement between them. They left him, rested that day, and fell asleep. 18/ That day Isaac was happy as he fell asleep on his bed. He fell asleep forever and died at the age of 180 years. He had completed 25 weeks of years[a] and five years. His two sons Esau and Jacob buried him.

Esau and Jacob Go to Their Homes (36:19–20)

19/ Esau went to the land of Mount Seir[b] and lived there, 20/ while Jacob lived on the mountain of Hebron, in the tower in the land of Canaan,[c] in the land of his father Abraham. He worshiped the Lord wholeheartedly and in line with the revealed commands according to the divisions of the times of his generation.

Jacob's Beloved Wife Leah Dies (36:21–24)

21/ His wife Leah died during the fourth year of the second week of the forty-fifth jubilee [2167]. He buried her in the twofold cave near his mother Rebekah, on the left of his grandmother Sarah's grave. 22/ All her sons and his sons came to mourn

---

a So 4Q223–224 2 iii:11; the Eth mss lack *of years*.

b *to the land of Mount Seir* is very likely the reading in 4Q223–224 2 iii:12; Eth has to *the land of Edom—to Mount Seir*.

c The phrase *in the land of Canaan* is in 4Q223–224 2 iii:13; it has dropped out of the Eth tradition because the next phrase starts with the same expression.

with him for his wife Leah and to comfort him regarding her because he was lamenting her. 23/ For he loved her very much from the time when her sister Rachel died because she was perfect and right in all her behavior and honored Jacob. In all the time that she lived with him he did not hear a harsh word from her mouth because she was gentle and possessed (the virtues of) peace, truthfulness, and honor. 24/ As he recalled all the things that she had done in her lifetime, he greatly lamented her because he loved her with all his heart and with all his person.

Hostilities Break Out between Esau and Jacob (Chapter 37)

Esau's Sons Want to Fight Jacob for the Birthright but Esau Opposes Their Plan (37:1–8)

37:1/ On the day that Isaac, the father of Jacob and Esau, died Esau's sons heard that Isaac had given the birthright[a] to his younger son Jacob. They became very angry. 2/ They quarreled with their father: "Why is it that when you are the older and Jacob the younger your father gave Jacob the birthright and deposed you?"[b] 3/ He said to them, "Because I gave[c] the right of the firstborn to Jacob in exchange for a little lentil broth. The day my father sent me to hunt game so that he could eat (it) and bless me, he came in a crafty way and brought in food and drink to my father. My father blessed him and put me under his control. 4/ Now our father has made us—me and him—swear that we will not seek harm, the one against his brother, and that we will continue in (a state of) mutual love and peace, each with his brother, so that we should not corrupt our behavior."[d]

---

a Lat appears to read something like *the larger and more honored part*. In v 2 it renders *birthright* as the *larger part*.

b Lat has *made you inferior*.

c So Lat and Syr; Eth reads *sold*.

d At *corrupt our behavior* Lat has *practice what is wrong toward one another*.

5/ They said to him, "We will not listen to you by making peace with him because our strength is greater than his strength, and we are stronger than he is. We will go against him, kill him, and destroy his sons. If you do not go with us, we will harm you, too. 6/ Now listen to us: let us send to Aram, Philistia, Moab, and Ammon; and let us choose for ourselves select men who are brave in battle. Then let us go against him, make war with him, and uproot him from the earth before he gains strength." 7/ Their father said to them, "Do not go and do not make war with him so that you may not fall before him." 8/ They said to him, "Is this not the very way you have acted from your youth until today. You are putting your neck beneath his yoke. We will not listen to what you are saying."

Esau's Sons Assemble an Army of Foreign Mercenaries (37:9–10)

9/ So they sent to Aram and to their father's friend Aduram. Together with them they hired for themselves 1,000 fighting men, select warriors. 10/ There came to them from Moab and from the Ammonites 1,000 select men who were hired; from the Philistines 1,000 select warriors; from Edom and the Horites 1,000 select fighters, and from the Kittim[a] strong warriors.

Esau Changes His Mind and Agrees to Attack Jacob (37:11–13)

11/ They said to their father, "Go out; lead them. Otherwise we will kill you." 12/ He was filled with anger and wrath when he saw that his sons were forcing him to go in front in order to lead them to his brother Jacob. 13/ But he remembered all the bad things that were hidden in his mind against his brother Jacob, and he did not remember the oath that he had sworn to his father and mother not to seek harm against Jacob throughout his entire lifetime.

---

a The Eth form could also be interpreted as *Hittites*.

Jacob Is Surprised by the Attack and Has an Unpleasant Exchange with Esau (37:14–23)

14/ During all this time, Jacob was unaware that they were coming to him for battle. He, for his part, was mourning for his wife until they approached him near the tower with 4,000 warriors. 15/ The people of Hebron sent word to him: "Your brother has just now come against you to fight you with 4,000 men who have swords buckled on and are carrying shields and weapons." They told him because they loved Jacob more than Esau, since Jacob was a more generous and kind man than Esau. 16/ But Jacob did not believe (it) until they came near the tower. 17/ Then he closed the gates of the tower, stood on the top, and spoke with his brother Esau. He said, "It is a fine consolation that you have come to give me for my wife who has died. Is this the oath that you swore to your father and your mother twice before he[a] died? You have violated the oath and were condemned in the hour when you swore (it) to your father."

18/ Then Esau said in reply to him, "Neither humankind nor serpents[b] have a true oath that they, once they have sworn, have sworn (it as valid) forever. Every day they desire harm for one another, how to kill his enemy and opponent. 19/ You hate me and my sons forever. There is no observing of brotherly ties with you. 20/ Listen to what I have to say to you. If a pig changes its hide and makes its hair limp like wool; and horns like the horns of a ram and sheep go out on its head, then I will observe brotherly ties with you. The breasts have been separated from their mother,[c] for you have not been a brother to me. 21/ If wolves make peace with lambs so that they do not eat them or injure them; and if they have resolved to treat them well, then there will be peace in my mind for you. 22/ If a lion becomes the friend of a bull and a confidant,[d] and if it is harnessed together with it in a yoke

---

a Some Eth copies "correct" to *they*, and Syr has *their (death)*.

b So 4Q223–224 2 iv:4; Eth and Syr read general words for *animals* (*Jubilees 22–50*, 973).

c For the various readings of this clause, see *Jubilees 22–50*, 974.

d The reading follows 4Q223–224 2 iv:10. Eth and Syr lack *the friend of* and *confidant*.

and plows (as) one yoke, then I will make peace with you. 23/ If the ravens turn white like a pelican,[a] then know that I love you and will make peace with you. (As for) you—be uprooted and your children are being uprooted. There is to be no peace for you."

Jacob Orders a Strike against Esau and His Army (37:24–25)

24/ When Jacob saw that he was adversely inclined toward him from his mind and his entire self so that he could kill him and (that) he was coming and bounding along like a boar that comes upon the spear that pierces it and kills it but does not pull back from it, 25/ then he told his sons[b] and his servants to attack him and his companions.

War between Esau and Jacob and an Edomite King List (Chapter 38)

The War between the Forces of Jacob and Esau (38:1–14)

38:1/ After this Judah spoke to his father Jacob and said to him, "Draw your bow, father; shoot your arrow; strike the enemy; and kill the foe. May you have the strength because we will not kill your brother, since he is your brother[c] and he is similar to you, and, in our estimation, he is like you in honor." 2/ Jacob then stretched his bow, shot an arrow, struck[d] his brother Esau on his right breast,[e] and killed him. 3/ He shot a second arrow and hit Aduran the Aramean on his left breast; he drove him back and killed him. 4/ After this Jacob's sons—they and their servants—went out, dividing themselves to the four sides of the tower. 5/ Judah went out first. Naphtali and Gad were with him, and 50 servants were with

---

 a The Eth copies have *rāzā*, a kind of bird of uncertain identification.
 b So Heb Syr; Eth reads *his own/his people*.
 c The clause is lacking in Eth.
 d So Syr and Midrash Wayyissaʻu; Eth *pierced*.
 e Eth lacks the prepositional phrase which Lat Syr support; there is space for it on 4Q223–224 2 iv:19.

them on the south side of the tower. They killed everyone whom they found in front of them. No one at all escaped from them. 6/ Levi, Dan, and Asher went out on the east side of the tower, and 50 were with them. They killed the Moabite and Ammonite bands.[a] 7/ Reuben, Issachar, and Zebulun went out on the north side of the tower,[b] and their 50 with them. They too[c] killed the Philistine fighting men. 8/ Simeon, Benjamin, and Enoch—Reuben's son—went out on the west side of the tower, and their 50 with them. Of (the people of) Edom and the Horites they killed 400 strong warriors, and 600 ran away.[d] Esau's four sons ran away with them. They left their slain father[e] thrown[f] on the hill that is in Adoraim. 9/ Jacob's sons pursued them as far as Mount Seir, while Jacob buried his brother on the hill that is in Adoraim and then returned to the tower.[g] 10/ Jacob's sons besieged Esau's sons in Mount Seir. They bowed their neck to become servants for Jacob's sons. 11/ They sent to their father (to ask) whether they should make peace with them or kill them. 12/ Jacob sent word to his sons to make peace. So they made peace with them and placed the yoke of servitude on them so that they should pay tribute to Jacob and his sons for all time. 13/ They continued paying tribute to Jacob until the day that he went down to Egypt. 14/ The Edomites have not extricated themselves from the yoke of servitude that Jacob's sons imposed[h] on them until today.

The Kings Who Ruled in Edom (38:15–24)

15/   These are the kings who ruled in Edom—before a king ruled the Israelites—until today in the land of Edom. 16/ Balak,

---

    a This appears to be the reading in 4Q221 6 2; Eth Lat have *warriors*.
    b Lat omits the prepositional phrase.
    c Eth lacks *too* which is present in Lat.
    d Lat lacks the verb.
    e At *their slain father* Lat reads *the body of their father*.
    f Eth *as he fell*.
    g Eth *his house*.
    h For the strange reading *twelve* in most Eth mss, see *Jubilees 22–50*, 991.

son of Be'or, became king in Edom. The name of his city was Danaba. 17/ After Balak died, Yobab son of Zara who was from Bosir became king in his place. 18/ After Yobab died, Asam who was from Mount Teman became king in his place. 19/ After Asam died, Adat son of Bared who slaughtered Midian in the field of Moab became king in his place. The name of his city was Awutu. 20/ After Adat died, Saloman who was from Emaseqa became king in his place. 21/ After Saloman died, Saul who was from the river Raabot became king in his place. 22/ After Saul died, Baelunan son of Akbur became king in his place. 23/ After Baelunan son of Akbur died, Adat became king in his place. His wife's name was Maytabit, daughter of Matrit, daughter of Metabedezaab. 24/ These are the kings who ruled in the land of Edom.

The Humble Beginnings of Joseph's Career in Egypt (Chapter 39)

Jacob in Canaan (39:1–2ab)

39:1/ Jacob lived in the land where his father had wandered as a foreigner—the land of Canaan. 2ab/ This is the history of Jacob. When Joseph was 17 years of age, they brought him down to Egypt.

Joseph's Success in Potiphar's House (39:2c–4)

2c/ Pharaoh's eunuch Potiphar, the chief cook, bought him. 3/ He put Joseph in charge of his entire house. The Lord's blessing was (present) in the Egyptian's house because of Joseph. The Lord made everything that he did succeed for him. 4/ The Egyptian <u>placed</u> everything before Joseph[a] because he noticed that the Lord was with him and that <u>God made</u> everything that he did <u>succeed</u> for him.

---

a 4Q221 7 1 may not have space enough to include the name rather than just the pronoun *him*.

Joseph and Potiphar's Wife (39:5–11)

5/ Now Joseph was well formed and very[a] handsome. The wife of his master looked up at him,[b] saw Joseph, loved him, and pleaded with him to sleep with her. 6/ But he did not surrender himself. He remembered the Lord and what his father Jacob would read to him from the words of Abraham—that no one is to commit adultery with a woman who has a husband; that there is a death penalty that has been ordained for him in heaven before the Most High God. The sin will be entered regarding him in the eternal books forever before the Lord. 7/ Joseph remembered what he had said and refused to sleep with her. 8/ She pleaded with him for one year and a second, but he refused to listen to her. 9/ She *grasped*[c] him and held on to him in the house to compel him to sleep with her. She closed the door[d] of the house and held on to him. He left his clothes in her hands, broke[e] the door, and ran away from her to the outside. 10/ When that woman saw that he would not sleep with her,[f] she accused him falsely to his master: "Your Hebrew slave whom you love wanted to force me so that he could sleep with me. When I shouted, he ran outside, left his clothes in my hands when I grabbed him by his clothes, and broke the bolt."[g] 11/ When the Egyptian saw Joseph's clothes and the broken door, he believed what his wife said. He put Joseph in prison in the place where the prisoners of the king were held.

---

a 4Q221 7 2 may not have space for *very*.

b 4Q221 7 3 very likely reads *at him*; Eth lacks the prepositional phrase.

c For the difficulties with the readings in Heb Lat and Eth, see *Jubilees 22–50*, 1004.

d If a small fragment is correctly placed, 4Q221 7 11 reads *gate/entrance* rather than *door*. Lat has *doors*.

e Lat has *opened*.

f 4Q223–224 2 v:2 and Eth agree in reading the clause; Lat has *he had defied her*.

g 4Q223–224 2 v:5 (space considerations) and Lat support a reference to *his clothes* here, while Eth lacks it. The translation *bolt* rests on a better reading of the partially preserved word in 4Q223–224 2 v:5 than the one rendered *door* in *Jubilees 22–50*, 1003 (see the textual note on 1005).

Joseph Succeeds in Prison (39:12–13)

12/ While he was there in prison, the Lord gave Joseph a favorable reception before the chief of the prison guards and a kind reception before him because he saw that the Lord was with him and that the Lord was making everything that he did succeed for him. 13/ He left everything to him. The chief of the prison guards knew nothing at all about his affairs because Joseph would do everything and the Lord would bring (it) to completion. He remained there for two years.

Joseph Successfully Interprets Two Dreams (39:14–18)

14/ At that time Pharaoh, the king of Egypt, became angry at two of his eunuchs—the chief butler and the chief baker. He put them in prison, in the house of the chief cook, in the prison where Joseph was held. 15/ The chief of the prison guards appointed Joseph to serve them. So he would serve in their presence. 16/ Both of them—the chief butler and the chief baker—had a dream and told it to Joseph. 17/ Things turned out for them just as he interpreted for them. Pharaoh restored the chief butler to his cupbearing,[a] but he hanged the baker as Joseph had interpreted for him. 18/ The chief butler forgot Joseph in prison although he had informed him (about) what would happen to him. He did not remember to tell Pharaoh what Joseph had told him because he forgot.

Joseph Interprets Pharaoh's Dreams and Becomes Ruler of Egypt (Chapter 40)

Pharaoh's Dreams and Joseph's Appointment as Second Ruler in Egypt (40:1–7)

40:1/ At that time Pharaoh had two dreams in one night about the subject of the famine that would come on the whole land. When he awakened, he summoned all the dream interpret-

---

a 4Q223–224 2 v:15 seems to preserve the first two consonants of *his cupbearing*; Eth reads *his work/job* and Lat has *his place*.

ers who were in Egypt and the enchanters. He told them his two dreams, but they were unable to interpret[a] them. 2/ Then the chief butler remembered Joseph. After he had told the king about him, he was brought from prison and he related the dreams in his presence. 3/ He interpreted[b] them in Pharaoh's presence—that his two dreams were one. He said to him, "Seven years are coming (in which there will be) abundance in the entire land of Egypt, but afterwards there will be a seven-year famine, the like of which has never been in the entire land. 4/ So now let Pharaoh appoint officers[c] throughout the entire land of Egypt and let them collect each city's food in the city during the period of the years of abundance.[d] Then there will be food for the seven years of famine, and the land will not perish because of the famine, since it will be very severe." 5/ God gave Joseph a favorable and kind reception before Pharaoh. Pharaoh said to his servants, "We will not find[e] a man as wise and knowledgeable as this man, for the spirit of God is with him." 6/ He appointed him as the second (in command) in his entire kingdom, gave him authority over all the land of Egypt, and allowed him to ride on Pharaoh's second chariot. 7/ He dressed him with clothing made of linen and put a gold chain on his neck. He made a proclamation before him and said, "Il il and abirer." He put the signet ring on his hand and made him ruler over his entire household. He made him great and said to him, "I will not be greater than you except with regard to the throne only."

Joseph's Just Rule over Egypt (40:8–13)

8/ So Joseph became ruler over the entire land of Egypt. All of Pharaoh's princes, all of his servants, and all who were doing

---

a Eth has *understand*.

b Eth reads *said*.

c Heb (partially preserved) and Lat agree on the term, but Eth has a puzzling reading that has not yet been explained. The strange term is also in an odd place in the Eth sentence (*Jubilees 22–50*, 1020).

d At *during the period of the years of abundance*, Lat reads *and store it during the seven years of abundance*.

e Lat phrases the clause as a question: *Will we be able to find?* See Gen 41:38.

the king's work loved him because he conducted himself in a just way. He was not arrogant, proud, or partial, nor did he accept bribes because he was ruling all the people of the land in a just way. 9/ The land of Egypt lived in harmony before Pharaoh because of Joseph for the Lord was with him. He gave him a favorable and kind reception for all his family before all who knew him and who heard reports about him. Pharaoh's rule was just, and there was no satan or any evil one. 10/ The king named Joseph Sefantifanes and gave Joseph as a wife the daughter of Potiphar, the daughter of the priest of Heliopolis—the chief cook. 11/ On the day when Joseph took up his position with Pharaoh he was 30 years of age when he took up his position with Pharaoh.[a] 12/ Isaac died that year. Things turned out just as Joseph had reported about the interpretation of his two dreams, just as he had reported to him. There were seven years of abundance in the whole land of Egypt. The land of Egypt was most productive: one measure (would produce) 1,800 measures. 13/ Joseph collected (each) city's food in the city until it was so full of wheat that it was impossible to count or measure it because of its quantity.

Judah and Tamar (Chapter 41)

Judah's Sons and Tamar (41:1–7)

41:1/ In the forty-fifth jubilee, the second week during the second year [2165], Judah took as a wife for his firstborn Er one of the Aramean women whose name was Tamar. 2/ He hated (her) and did not sleep with her because his mother was a Canaanite woman and he wanted to marry someone from his mother's tribe. But his father Judah did not allow him. 3/ This Er, Judah's firstborn, was evil, and the Lord killed him. 4/ Then Judah said to his brother Onan, "Go in to your brother's wife, perform the levirate duty for her, and produce descendants for your brother." 5/ Onan knew that the descendants would not be his but his brother's, so he entered

---

a Possibly the last clause should be read with v 12 (*Jubilees 22–50*, 1031).

the house of his brother's wife and poured out the semen on the ground. In the Lord's estimation it was an evil act,[a] and he killed him. 6/ So Judah said to his daughter-in-law Tamar, "Remain in your father's house as a widow until my son Selom grows up. Then I will give you to him as a wife." 7/ He grew up, but Judah's wife Bedsuel did not allow her son Selom to marry her. Judah's wife Bedsuel died during the fifth year of this week [2168].

Judah and Tamar (41:8–21)

Tamar Misleads Judah (41:8–12)

8/ In its sixth year [2169] Judah went up to shear his sheep in Timnah. Tamar was told, "Your father-in-law is now going up to shear his sheep in Timnah." 9/ Then she put aside her widow's clothing from herself,[b] put on a veil,[c] beautified herself, and sat down at the gate near the road to Timnah. 10/ As Judah was going along, he found her and supposed that she was a prostitute. He said to her, "Let me come in to you." She said to him, "Come in." So he came in. 11/ She said to him, "Give me my fee." He said to her, "I have nothing with me except the ring on my finger, my neck chain, and my staff that is in my hand." 12/ She said to him, "Give them to me until you send me my fee." He said to her, "I will send you a kid." He gave them to her. After he was with her,[d] she became pregnant by him.

Tamar Disappears (41:13–15)

13/ Then Judah went to his sheep, but she went to her father's house.[e] 14/ He sent the kid through his Adullamite shep-

---

   a The clause could be rendered *he was evil*. Syr, which differs from Eth considerably in the general context, has *in this he did something evil*.

   b Both Lat and Syr read the phrase, but Eth lacks it.

   c So Eth Syr, but Lat has *the best clothes*.

   d So Lat Syr; Eth lacks the clause.

   e Lat Syr lack the clause, but Eth has it. It is presupposed by Jub 41:17 where Eth Lat and Syr attest it.

herd, but he did not find her. He asked the men of the area, "Where is the prostitute who was here?" They said to him, "There is no prostitute here, nor do we have any prostitute with us."[a] 15/ He returned and told him, "I did not find her,[b] and when I asked the men of the area they said to me, 'There is no prostitute here.'" Judah said, "Let her keep them[c] so that we may not become the object of mockery."[d]

The Truth Emerges and Twins Are Born (41:16–21)

16/ When she reached three months, she was visibly pregnant. Judah was told, "Your daughter-in-law Tamar has now become pregnant through prostitution." 17/ Judah went to her father's house and said to her father and brothers, "Bring her out and let her be burned[e] because she has done something impure in Israel." 18/ When she was brought out to be burned, she sent the ring, the neck chain, and the staff to her father-in-law and said, "Recognize whose these are because I am pregnant by him." 19/ Judah recognized them and said, "Tamar has been more just than I; therefore, do not burn her." 20/ For this reason she was not given to Selom, and he did not approach her again. 21/ Afterwards she was pregnant and gave birth to two boys—Perez and Zerah—during the seventh year of this second week [2170].

The Seven Years of Abundance End (41:22)

22/ Following this the seven years of copious harvest (about) which Joseph had told Pharaoh were completed.

---

    a Eth includes the sentence, but Lat reads only *There is no prostitute here with us.* Syr has *There is no prostitute here.*
    b Eth phrases the clause as indirect speech (*Jubilees 22–50*, 1035).
    c For the Eth reading, see *Jubilees 22–50*, 1035.
    d Lat reads *so that she does not mock us.*
    e Eth has *let them burn her.*

Legal Issues (41:23–28)

Judah's Remorse and Pardon (41:23–25)

23/ Judah knew that what he had done was evil because he had lain with his daughter-in-law. In his own view he considered it evil, and he knew that he had done wrong and erred, for he had uncovered his son's covering. He began to lament and plead before the Lord because of his sin. 24/ We told him in a dream that it would be forgiven for him because he had pleaded very much and because he had lamented and did not do (it) again. 25/ He had forgiveness because he turned from his sin and from his ignorance, for the sin was a great one before our God. Anyone who acts in this way—anyone who sleeps with his daughter-in-law[a]—is to be burned in fire so that he burns in it because impurity and contamination have come on them. They are to be burned.

The Law for Israel (41:26–28)

26/ Now you order the Israelites that there is to be no impurity among them, for anyone who lies with his daughter-in-law or his mother-in-law has done something that is impure. They are to burn the man who lay with her and the woman. Then anger and punishment will cease from Israel. 27/ We told Judah that his two sons had not lain with her. For this reason his descendants were established for another generation and would not be uprooted. 28/ For in his integrity he had gone and demanded punishment because Judah had wanted to burn her on the basis of the law that Abraham had commanded his children.

Joseph's Brothers Travel to Egypt (Chapter 42)

The Famine Begins (42:1–3)

42:1/ During the first year of the third week of the forty-fifth jubilee [2171], the famine began to come to the land. The rain

---

a Many Eth mss read *mother-in-law*.

refused to be given to the earth because there was nothing that was coming down. 2/ The earth became unproductive, but in the land of Egypt there was food because Joseph had gathered the grain in the land during the seven years of copious harvest and kept it. 3/ When the Egyptians came to Joseph so that he would give them food, he opened the storehouses where the grain was. He gave (it) to them to eat in the first year[a] and sold (it) to the people of the land in exchange for money.[b]

The Brothers Make Their First Trip to Egypt, Encounter a Harsh Joseph, and Return Home (42:4–12)

4/ But the famine was very severe in the land of Canaan.[c] Jacob heard that there was food in Egypt, so he sent his ten sons to get food for him in Egypt. But he did not send Benjamin. They arrived with those who were coming to Egypt.[d] 5/ Joseph recognized them, but they did not recognize him. He spoke with them, asked them questions,[e] and said to them, "Are you not spies?[f] You have come to investigate the paths of the land." He then imprisoned them. 6/ Afterwards he sent again and summoned[g] them. He detained only Simeon and sent his nine brothers away. 7/ He filled their sacks with grain and returned their money to them in their sacks. But they did not know (this).[h] 8/ He ordered them to bring their youngest brother because they had told him that their father was alive and their youngest brother (also). 9/ They went up from the land of Egypt and came to the

---

   a *the grain was. He gave (it) to them to eat in the first year* is the Lat reading. Eth has *the grain of the first year*.
   b Lat lacks *in exchange for money* (see Gen 41:56).
   c Eth lacks the sentence, but Lat reads it.
   d Lat words the sentence as *Jacob's ten sons arrived in Egypt*.
   e For the first words of the sentence Lat reads *Joseph addressed them harshly* (*Jubilees 22–50*, 1057–58).
   f Lat lacks the question.
   g Lat reads *summoned*; Eth reads *released*.
   h Lat omits from *in their sacks* to the end of the verse.

land of Canaan. They told their father everything that had happened to them and how the ruler of the country had spoken harshly with them and was holding Simeon until they should bring Benjamin. 10/ Jacob said, "You have deprived me of children. Joseph does not exist nor does Simeon exist, and you are going to take Benjamin. Your wickedness has come upon me." 11/ He said, "My son will not go with you. Perhaps he would become ill. For their mother gave birth to two; one has died and this one, too, you will take from me. Perhaps he would catch a fever on the way. Then you would bring down my old age in sorrow to Sheol."[a] 12/ For he saw that their money was returned—each one in his purse—and he was afraid to send him for this reason.

The Famine Grows More Severe and the Egyptians Cope by Imitating Joseph (42:13-14)

13/ Now the famine grew increasingly severe in the land of Canaan and in every land except the land of Egypt because many Egyptians had kept their seed in storage places after they saw Joseph collecting grain, placing it in storehouses, and keeping (it) for the years of the famine. 14/ The Egyptians fed themselves with it during the first year of the famine.

Jacob Agrees to Send Benjamin with His Brothers on Their Second Trip to Egypt (42:15-20)

15/ When Israel saw that the famine was very severe in the land and (that) there was no relief, he said to his sons, "Go, return, and get us (some) food so that we may not die." 16/ But they said, "We will not go. If our youngest brother does not come with us, we will not go." 17/ Israel saw that if he did not send him with them they would all die because of the famine. 18/ Then Reuben said, "Put him under my control. If I do not bring him back to you, kill my two sons for his life." But

---

[a] The word *Sheol* (Gen 42:38) was interpreted as *death* in Eth and as *the depths* in Lat.

he said to him, "He will not go with you." 19/ Then Judah approached and said, "Send him with us. If I do not bring him back to you, then let me be guilty before you throughout my entire lifetime." 20/ So he sent him with them during the second year of this week [2172], on the first of the month. They arrived in the country of Egypt with all who were going (there) and (had) their gifts in their hands: stacte, almonds, terebinth nuts, and honeycombs.

The Brothers Meet Joseph Who Devises a Plot to Test Them (42:21–25)

21/ They arrived and stood in front of Joseph. When he saw his brother Benjamin, he recognized him and said to them, "Is this your youngest brother?" They said to him, "He is." He said, "May God be gracious to you, my son." 22/ He sent him into his house and brought Simeon out to them. He prepared a dinner for them. They presented him with his gifts that they had brought in their hands. 23/ They ate in front of him. He gave portions to all of them, but Benjamin's share was seven times larger than the share of any of them. 24/ They ate and drank. Then they got up and stayed with their donkeys. 25/ Joseph conceived of a plan by which he would know their thoughts—whether there were peaceful thoughts between them. He said to the man who was in charge of his house, "Fill all their sacks with food for them and return their money to them in their containers; put the cup with which I drink in the sack of the youngest—the silver cup—and send them away."

Joseph Tests His Brothers and Reveals His Identity (Chapter 43)

The Cup as an Instrument for Testing Relations between the Brothers (43:1–13)

Placing and Finding the Cup in Benjamin's Sack (43:1–8a)

43:1/ He did as Joseph told him. He filled their sacks completely with food for them and placed their money in their sacks.

He put the cup in Benjamin's sack. 2/ Early in the morning they went (off). But when they had left that place, Joseph said to the man of his house, "Pursue them. Run and reprimand them as follows: 'You have repaid me with evil instead of good. You have stolen from me the silver cup with which my master drinks.' Bring their youngest brother back to me and bring him quickly, before I go out to the place where I rule." 3/ He ran after them and spoke to them in line with this message. 4/ They said to him, "Heaven forbid that your servants should do such a thing and should steal any container from the house of your master. Your servants have brought back from the land of Canaan the money that we found in our sacks the first time. 5/ How, then, should we steal any container? We and our sacks are here. Make a search, and anyone of us in whose sack you find the cup is to be killed, while we and our donkeys are to serve your master." 6/ He said to them, "(That) is not the way it will be. I will take as a servant only the man with whom I find it, and you may go safely to your home." 7/ As he was searching among their containers, he began with the oldest and ended with the youngest. It was found in Benjamin's sack. 8/ They tore their clothing, loaded their donkeys, and returned to the city.

Confrontation with Joseph (43:8b–10)

When they arrived at Joseph's house, all of them bowed to him with their faces to the ground. 9/ Joseph said to them, "You have done an evil thing." They said, "What are we to say and what shall we say in our defense. Our master has discovered the crime of his servants. We ourselves and our donkeys, too, are our master's servants." 10/ Joseph said to them, "As for me, I fear God. As for you, go to your houses, but your brother is to be enslaved because you have done something evil. Do you not know that a man takes pleasure in his cup as I do in this cup? And you stole it from me."

Judah's Speech (43:11–13)

11/ Then Judah said, "*Please*,[a] master, allow me, your servant, to say something in my master's hearing. His mother gave birth to two brothers for your servant our father. One has gone away and been lost; no one has found him. He alone is left of his mother('s children). And your servant our father loves him and his life is tied together with the life of this one. 12/ If we go to your servant our father and if the young man is not with us, then he would die and we would bring our father down in sorrow to death. 13/ Rather, I your servant will remain in place of the child as a servant of my master. Let the young man go with his brothers because I took responsibility for him from your servant our father. If I do not bring him back, your servant will be guilty to our father forever."

Joseph Reveals His Identity (43:14–20)

14/ When Joseph saw that the minds of all of them were in harmony one with the other for good (ends), he was unable to control himself, and he told them that he was Joseph. 15/ He spoke with them in the Hebrew language. He wrapped his arms around their necks and cried. But they did not recognize him and began to cry. 16/ Then he said to them, "Do not cry about me. Quickly bring my father to me and let *him* see *me* before *he*[b] dies, while my brother Benjamin also looks on. 17/ For this is now the second year of the famine and there are still five more years without harvest, without fruit (growing on) trees, and without plowing. 18/ You and your households come down quickly so that you may not die in the famine. Do not worry about your property because the Lord sent me first before you to arrange matters so that many

---

a Eth reads *upon me* which is a literal translation of a Hebrew particle meaning *please* (Gen 44:18).

b For the three italicized pronouns, almost all Eth mss read *me, him, I*. Jacob's death is clearly the one under consideration, not Joseph's, hence the emendations.

people may remain alive. 19/ Tell my father that I am still alive. You now see that the Lord has made me like a father to Pharaoh and to rule in his household and over the entire land of Egypt. 20/ Tell my father about all my splendor and all the wealth and splendor that the Lord has given me."

The Return Trip and Announcement of the Good News to Jacob (43:21–24)

21/ By personal command of Pharaoh he gave them wagons and provisions for the trip, and he gave all of them colored clothing and silver. 22/ To their father he sent clothing, silver, and donkeys that were carrying grain. Then he sent them away. 23/ They went up and told their father that Joseph was alive and that he was having grain distributed to all the peoples of the earth and ruling over the entire land of Egypt. 24/ Their father did not believe (it) because he was disturbed in his thoughts. But after he saw the wagons that Joseph had sent, his spirit revived and he said, "It is enough for me that Joseph is alive. Let me go down and see him before I die."

The Descent to Egypt by Jacob and His Family (Chapter 44)

From Hebron to the Well of the Oath (44:1–6)

44:1/ Israel set out from *Hebron*,[a] from his house, on the first of the third month. He went by way of the well of the oath and offered a sacrifice to the God of his father Isaac on the seventh of this month. 2/ When Jacob remembered the dream that he had seen in Bethel, he was afraid to go down to Egypt. 3/ But as he was thinking about sending word to Joseph that he should come to him and that he would not go down, he remained there for seven days on the chance that he would see a vision (about) whether he should remain or

---

[a] The Eth mss read *Haran*, which is an obvious mistake, judging by the context (Jub 44:6 and 46:9–10).

go down. 4/ He celebrated the harvest festival—the firstfruits of grain—with old grain because in all the land of Canaan there was not even a handful of seed in the land since the famine affected all the animals, the cattle, the birds, and humanity as well.

5/ On the sixteenth the Lord appeared to him and said to him, "Jacob, Jacob." He said, "Yes?" He said to him, "I am the God of your fathers—the God of Abraham and Isaac. Do not be afraid to go down to Egypt because I will make you into a great nation there. 6/ I will go down with you and will lead you (back). You will be buried in this land, and Joseph will place his hands on your eyes. Do not be afraid; go down to Egypt."

From the Well of the Oath toward Goshen (44:7–10)

7/ His sons and grandsons set about loading their father and their property on the wagons. 8/ Israel set out from the well of the oath on the sixteenth day of this third month and went to the land of Egypt. 9/ Israel sent his son Judah in front of him to Joseph to examine the land of Goshen because Joseph had told his brothers to come there in order to live there so that they would be his neighbors. 10/ It was the best (place) in the land of Egypt and (it was) near him for each one and their cattle.[a]

The Seventy Who Descended to Egypt (44:11–34)

11/ These are the names of Jacob's children who went to Egypt with their father Jacob. 12/ Reuben, Israel's firstborn, and these are the names of his sons: Hanoch, Pallu, Hezron, and Carmi—five; 13/ Simeon and his sons, and these are the names of his sons: Jemuel, Jamin, Ohad, Jachin, Zohar, and Shaul, the son of the Phoenician woman—seven; 14/ Levi and his sons, and these are the names of his sons: Gershon, Kohath, and Merari—four; 15/ Judah and his sons, and these

---

a For the end of the verse, see *Jubilees 22–50*, 1088.

are the names of his sons: Shelah, Perez, and Zerah—four; 16/ Issachar and his sons, and these are the names of his sons: Tola, Puvah, Jashub, and Shimron—five; 17/ Zebulun and his sons, and these are the names of his sons: Sered, Elon, and Jahleel—four; 18/ These are Jacob's sons and their sons to whom Leah gave birth for Jacob in Mesopotamia—six and their one sister Dinah. All of the persons of Leah's sons and their sons who went with their father Jacob to Egypt were twenty-nine. And, as their father Jacob was with them, they were thirty.

19/ The sons of Zilpah, the maid of Jacob's wife Leah, to whom she gave birth for Jacob were Gad and Asher. 20/ These are the names of their sons who went with him into Egypt. Gad's sons: Ziphion, Haggi, Shuni, Ezbon, [Eri],[a] Areli, and Arodi—eight. 21/ The children of Asher: Imnah, Ishvah, [Ishvi],[b] Beriah, and their one sister Serah—*six*. 22/ All the persons were fourteen, and all those of Leah were forty-four.

23/ The sons of Rachel who was Jacob's wife were Joseph and Benjamin. 24/ Before his father came to Egypt children, to whom Asenath—the daughter of Potiphar, the priest of Heliopolis—gave birth for him, were born to Joseph in Egypt: Manasseh and Ephraim—three. 25/ The sons of Benjamin were: Bela, Becher, Ashbel, Gera, Naaman, Ehi, Rosh, Muppim, Huppim, and Ard—eleven. 26/ All the persons of Rachel were fourteen.

27/ The sons of Bilhah, the maid of Jacob's wife Rachel, to whom she gave birth for Jacob were Dan and Naphtali. 28/ These are the names of their sons who went with them to Egypt. The sons of Dan were: Hushim, Samon, Asudi, Iyaka, and Salomon—six. 29/ They died in Egypt during the year in which they came (there). Only Hushim was left to Dan. 30/ These are the names of Naphtali's sons: Jahzeel, Guni, Jezer, Shillem, and Ev. 31/ Ev, who was born after the years of the famine, died in Egypt. 32/ All those of Rachel were twenty-six.

---

a The name has dropped out of the list. Without it the total at the end of the line would be *seven*, not *eight*.

b Without the name, the total at the end of the line would be one too high.

33/ All the persons of Jacob who entered Egypt were seventy persons. So all of these sons and grandsons of his were seventy, and five who died in Egypt before they married. They had no children. 34/ Judah's two sons Er and Onan had died in the land of Canaan. They had no children. The sons of Israel buried those who died, and they were placed among the seventy nations.

Reunion of the Family and Death of Jacob (Chapter 45)

The Reunion of Jacob and Joseph (45:1–5)

45:1/ Israel went into the land of Egypt, into the land of Goshen, on the first of the fourth month during the second year of the third week of the forty-fifth jubilee [2172]. 2/ When Joseph came to meet his father Jacob in the land of Goshen, he wrapped his arms around his father's neck and cried. 3/ Israel said to Joseph, "Now let me die after I have seen you. Now may the Lord, the God of Israel, the God of Abraham, and the God of Isaac—who has not withheld his kindness and his mercy from his servant Jacob—be blessed. 4/ It is enough for me that I have seen your face while I am alive, because the vision that I saw in Bethel was certainly true. May the Lord my God be blessed forever and ever and may his name be blessed." 5/ Joseph and his brothers ate food and drank wine in front of their father. Jacob was extremely happy because in front of him he saw Joseph eating and drinking with his brothers. He blessed the Creator of all who had preserved him and preserved his twelve sons for him.

Joseph's Provisions for His Father and Brothers (45:6–7)

6/ As a gift Joseph gave his father and his brothers (the right) to live in the land of Goshen, that is, in Rameses; and (he gave) them all its districts that they would rule in Pharaoh's presence. Israel and his sons lived in the land of Goshen, the best part of the land of Egypt. Israel was 130 years of age when he came into Egypt. 7/ Joseph provided as much food for his father, his brothers, and also for their livestock as would be sufficient for them for the seven years of famine.

Joseph's Supervision of the Famine Relief (45:8–12)

8/ As the land of Egypt suffered from the famine, Joseph gained the whole land of Egypt for Pharaoh in exchange for food. He acquired the people, their cattle, and everything for Pharaoh.[a] 9/ When the years of the famine were completed, Joseph gave seed and food to the peoples who were in the land so that they could sow seed in the eighth year because the river had overflowed the entire land of Egypt. 10/ For during the seven years of the famine it had irrigated only a few places at the riverbank, but now it overflowed.[b] The Egyptians seeded the land, and it yielded good produce that year. 11/ That was the first year of the fourth week of the forty-fifth jubilee [2178]. 12/ Joseph took the king's fifth part of all that had been sown, and he left four parts for them for food and seed. Joseph made it a law for the land of Egypt until today.

Jacob's Last Days (45:13–16)

13/ Israel lived for 17 years in the land of Egypt. All of the time that he lived was three jubilees—147 years. He died during the fourth year of the fifth week of the forty-fifth jubilee [2188]. 14/ Israel blessed his sons before he died. He told them everything that would happen to them in the land of Egypt; and he informed them (about) what would happen to them at the end of time. He blessed them and gave Joseph two shares in the land. 15/ He slept with his fathers and was buried near his father Abraham in the double cave in the land of Canaan—in the grave that he had dug for himself in

---

a Almost all of the Eth mss make Pharaoh the subject of *acquired*. A few copies and Lat read the sentence as above (*Jubilees 22–50*, 1103–4).

b From *it had irrigated* through *but now it overflowed* the Eth mss read as translated here; Lat has *it had not overflowed and had irrigated only a few places at the riverbank*.

the double cave in the land of Hebron. 16/ He gave all his books and the books of his fathers to his son Levi so that he could preserve them and renew them for his sons until today.

From Harmony to Oppression (Chapter 46)

Harmonious Relations in Egypt (46:1–2)

46:1/ After the death of Jacob, the children of Israel became numerous in the land of Egypt. They became a populous nation, and all of them were of the same mind so that each one loved the other and each one helped the other. They became numerous and increased very much—even for ten weeks of years [= 70 years]—for all of Joseph's lifetime. 2/ There was no satan or any evil one throughout all of Joseph's lifetime that he lived after his father Jacob because all the Egyptians were honoring the children of Israel for all of Joseph's lifetime.

Deaths of the Twelve Brothers with Burials Delayed by Warfare (46:3–11)

3/ Joseph died when he was 110 years of age. He had lived for 17 years in the land of Canaan; for ten years he remained enslaved; he was in prison for three years; and for 80 years he was ruling the entire land of Egypt under Pharaoh. 4/ He died and all his brothers and all of that generation. 5/ Before he died he ordered the Israelites to take his bones along at the time when they would leave the land of Egypt. 6/ He made them swear about his bones because he knew that the Egyptians would surely not allow him to be brought out[a] and be buried in the land of Canaan on the day of his death, since Makamaron, the king of Canaan—while he was living in the land of Asur[b]—fought in the valley with the king of

---

a The translation *would surely not allow him to be brought out* reflects the Greek text. Here Eth has *would not again bring him out* (*Jubilees 22–50*, 1118).

b The Greek citation lacks the phrase between dashes.

Egypt and killed him there. He pursued the Egyptians as far as the borders of Egypt.[a] 7/ He was unable to enter because another new king ruled Egypt. He was stronger than he, so he returned to the land of Canaan[b] and the gates of Egypt were closed with no one entering or leaving Egypt.

8/ Joseph died in the forty-sixth jubilee, in the sixth week, during its second year [2242]. He was buried in the land of Egypt,[c] and all his brothers died after him. 9/ Then the king of Egypt went out to fight with the king of Canaan in the forty-seventh jubilee, in the second week, during its second year [2263]. The Israelites brought out all the bones of Jacob's sons except Joseph's bones. They buried them in the field of the double cave in the mountain. 10/ Many returned to Egypt but a few of them remained on the mountain of Hebron. Your father Amram remained with them.

11/ The king of Canaan conquered the king of Egypt and closed[d] the gates of Egypt.

The Egyptian King Initiates Oppressive Measures against the Israelites (46:12–16)

12/ He[e] conceived an evil plan against the Israelites in order to make them suffer. He said to the Egyptians: 13/ "The nation of the Israelites has now increased and become more numerous than we are. Come on, let us outwit them before they multiply. Let us make them suffer in slavery before war comes our way and they, too, fight against us. Otherwise they will unite with the enemy and leave our land because their mind(s) and face(s look) toward the land of Canaan." 14/ He appointed taskmasters over them to make them suffer in slavery. They built fortified cities for Pharaoh—Pithom and Rameses. They built every wall and all the fortifications

---

a For *the borders of Egypt* Eth reads *the gates of Ermon*.
b *so he returned to the land of Canaan* is lacking in the Greek citation.
c For *in the land of Egypt* the Greek citation reads *in the coffin in Egypt*.
d The Greek citation specifies that *the king of Egypt closed*.
e Lat reads *The king of Canaan*.

that had fallen down in the cities of Egypt. 15/ They were enslaving them by force, but however much they would make them suffer the more they would multiply and the more they would increase. 16/ The Egyptians considered the Israelites detestable.

From Moses's Birth to His Escape from Egypt (Chapter 47)

Moses's Birth and Rescue by Pharaoh's Daughter (47:1–8)

47:1/ During the seventh week, in the seventh year, in the forty-seventh jubilee [2303], your[a] father came from the land of Canaan. You were born during the fourth week, in its sixth year, in the forty-eighth jubilee [2330]. This was the time of distress for the Israelites. 2/ Pharaoh, the king of Egypt, had given orders regarding them that they were to throw their sons—every male who was born—into the river. 3/ They continued throwing (them in) for seven months until the time when you were born. Your mother hid you for three months. Then they told about her. 4/ She made a box for you, covered it with pitch and asphalt, and put it in the grass[b] at the riverbank. She put you in it for seven days. Your mother would come at night and nurse you, and during the day your sister Miriam would protect you from the birds. 5/ At that time Tarmuth, Pharaoh's daughter, went out to bathe in the river and heard you crying. She told her slaves[c] to bring you, so they brought you to her. 6/ She took you out of the box and pitied you. 7/ Then your sister said to her, "Should I go[d] and summon for you one of the Hebrew women who will care for and nurse this infant for you?" She said to her, "Go."

---

a Lat uses a third-person form here (*his*) and later in the verse (*he was born*), when second-person forms are needed.

b Lat lacks *in the grass*.

c Eth reads *her Hebrews* (feminine). Since Dillmann's first publication of Jubilees ("Jubiläen," 72 n. 80), the Eth form has been regarded as a confusion that arose in Greek Jubilees: *abrais* (*female servants*) was misread as *ebraiais* (*Hebrew women*).

d Lat does not present her words as a question but later adds *if you wish*.

8/ She went and summoned your mother Jochebed. She gave her wages and she took care of you.

Life at Home and in the Royal Court (47:9–10a)

9/ Afterwards, when you had grown up, you were brought to Pharaoh's *daughter*[a] and became her child. Your father Amram taught you (the art of) writing. After you had completed three weeks [= 21 years], he brought you into the royal court. 10/ You remained in the court for three weeks of years [= 21 years] until the time when you went from the royal court and saw the Egyptian beating your kinsman who was one of the Israelites.[b]

Danger and Flight from Egypt (47:10b–12)

You killed him and hid him in the sand. 11/ The next day you found two of the Israelites fighting. You said to the one who was mistreating (the other): "Why are you beating your brother?" 12/ He became angry and indignant and said, "Who appointed you as ruler and judge over us? Do you want to kill me as you killed the Egyptian?" Then you were afraid and ran away because of this matter.

Moses's Return to Egypt, the Plagues, and the Exodus (Chapter 48)

Moses to Midian and Back (48:1–3)

48:1/ During the sixth year of the third week of the forty-ninth jubilee [2372], you went and lived there[c] for five weeks and one year [= 36 years]. Then you returned to Egypt in the second week, during the second year in the fiftieth jubilee [2410].

---

a Eth mss read *house*, a mistake that goes back to a confusion between Heb *bt* (*daughter*) and *byt* (*house*).

b Lat lacks the relative clause.

c Lat reads *mad-* (the first letters of *Midian*) as in Exod 2:15.

2/ You know who spoke to you at Mount Sinai and what the prince of Mastema wanted to do to you while you were returning to Egypt—on the way at the shady fir tree.[a] 3/ Did he not wish with all his strength to kill you and to save the Egyptians from your power because he saw that you were sent to carry out punishment and revenge on the Egyptians?

Revenge through the Ten Plagues (48:4–8)

4/ I rescued you from his power. You performed the signs and miracles that you were sent to perform in Egypt against Pharaoh, all his house, his servants, and his nation. 5/ The Lord effected a great revenge against them on account of Israel. He struck them and killed them with blood, frogs, gnats, dog flies, bad sores that break out in boils; (and he struck) their cattle with death; and with hailstones—with these he annihilated everything that was growing for them; with locusts that ate whatever was left for them from the hail; with darkness; (and with the death of) their firstborn of men and cattle. The Lord took revenge on all their gods and burned them up. 6/ Everything was sent through you, before it was done, so that you should do (it). You were speaking with the king of Egypt and in front of all his servants and his people. 7/ Everything happened by your word. Ten great and severe punishments came to the land of Egypt so that you could take revenge on it for Israel. 8/ The Lord did everything for the sake of Israel and in accord with his covenant that he made with Abraham to take revenge on them just as they were enslaving them with force.

Defeat of Mastema and the Egyptians (48:9–19)

9/ The prince of Mastema would stand up against you and wish to make you fall into Pharaoh's power. He would help the Egyptian magicians and they would oppose (you) and perform in front of you. 10/ We permitted them to do evil

---

a For the different readings of the phrase, see *Jubilees 22–50*, 1148.

things, but we would not allow healings to be performed by them. 11/ When the Lord struck them with bad sores, they were unable to oppose (you) because we deprived them of (their ability) to perform any sign at all. 12/ Despite all the signs and miracles, the prince of Mastema was not shamed until he gained strength and cried out to the Egyptians to pursue you with all the Egyptian army—with their chariots, their horses—and with all the throng of the Egyptian people.

13/ I stood between you, the Egyptians, and the Israelites. We rescued the Israelites from his power and from the power of the people. The Lord brought them out through the middle of the sea as if on dry ground. 14/ All of the people whom he brought out to pursue the Israelites the Lord our God threw into the sea—to the depths of the abyss—in place of the Israelites, just as the Egyptians had thrown their sons into the river. He took revenge on 1,000,000 of them; 1,000 strong men and also officers[a] eager for battle perished for one infant of your people whom they had thrown into the river.

15/ On the fourteenth day, the fifteenth, the sixteenth, the seventeenth, and the eighteenth the prince of Mastema was bound and locked up behind the Israelites so that he could not accuse them. 16/ On the nineteenth day we released them[b] so that they could help the Egyptians and pursue the Israelites. 17/ He hardened their hearts and made them strong. They were made strong by the Lord our God so that he could strike the Egyptians and throw them into the sea. 18/ On the fourteenth day we bound him so that he could not accuse the Israelites on the day when they were requesting utensils and clothing from the Egyptians—utensils of silver, utensils of gold, and utensils of bronze; and so that they could plunder the Egyptians in return for the fact that they were made to work when they enslaved them by force. 19/ We did not bring the Israelites out of Egypt empty-handed.

---

a In *Jubilees 22–50*, 1149 there is a discussion of the term and the Heb word that probably underlies it.

b A couple of Eth copies read *him* and *he* (for *they*) in the result clause that follows.

The First Passover and the Laws of Passover (Chapter 49)

The Timing of Passover (49:1)

49:1/ Remember the commandments that the Lord gave you regarding the Passover so that you may celebrate it at its time on the fourteenth of the first month, that you may sacrifice it before evening, and so that they may eat it at night on the evening of the fifteenth from the time of sunset.

The First Passover (49:2–6)

2/ For on this night—it was the beginning of the festival and the beginning of joy—you were eating the Passover in Egypt when all the forces of Mastema were sent to kill every firstborn in the land of Egypt—from Pharaoh's firstborn to the firstborn of the captive slave girl at the millstone and to the cattle as well. 3/ This is the sign that the Lord gave[a] them: into each house on whose door they saw the blood of a year-old lamb, they were not to enter that house to kill but were to pass over (it) in order that all who were in the house would be spared because the sign of the blood was on its door. 4/ The Lord's forces did everything that the Lord ordered them. They passed over all the Israelites. The plague did not come on them to destroy any of them—from cattle to humans to dogs. 5/ The plague on Egypt was very great. There was no house in Egypt in which there was not a dead person, crying, and mourning. 6/ All Israel was eating the paschal meat, drinking the wine, and glorifying, blessing, and praising the Lord God of their fathers. They were ready to leave the Egyptian yoke and evil slavery.

The Proper Time for Celebrating Passover (49:7–15)

7/ Now you remember this day throughout all your lifetime. Celebrate it from year to year throughout all your lifetime, once

---

a The mss include and omit various words in the clause, while several read all of them (*Jubilees 22–50*, 1167).

a year on its day in accord with all of its law. Then you will not pass over a day from the day[a] or from month to month. 8/ For it is an eternal statute and it is engraved on the heavenly tablets regarding the Israelites that they are to celebrate it each and every year on its day, once a year, throughout their entire history. There is no temporal limit because it is ordained forever. 9/ The man who is pure but does not come to celebrate it on its prescribed day—to bring a sacrifice that is pleasing before the Lord and to eat and drink before the Lord on the day of his festival—that man who is pure and nearby is to be uprooted because he did not bring the Lord's sacrifice at its time. That man will bear responsibility for his own sin. 10/ The Israelites are to come and celebrate the Passover on its specific day—on the fourteenth of the first month—between the evenings, from the third part of the day until the third part of the night. For two parts of the day have been given for light and its third part for the evening. 11/ This is what the Lord commanded you—to celebrate it between the evenings. 12/ It is not to be sacrificed at any hour of the daylight but in the hour of the boundary of[b] the evening. They will eat it during the evening hour(s) until the third part of the night. Any of its meat that is left over from the third part of the night and beyond is to be burned. 13/ They are not to boil it in water nor eat it raw but roasted on a fire, cooked with care on a fire[c]—the head with its internal parts and its feet. They are to roast it on a fire. There will be no breaking of any bone in it because no bone of the Israelites will be broken.[d]

14/ Therefore the Lord ordered the Israelites to celebrate the Passover on its specific day. No bone of it is to be broken because it is a festal day and a day that has been commanded. From it there is to be no passing over a day from the day or

---

a For the textual issues with the sentence to this point, see *Jubilees 22–50*, 1167.

b At *in the hour of the boundary of*, Lat has *in*.

c Lat has *you will eat it carefully*.

d At *because* through *broken*, Lat reads *there is to be no distress among the Israelites on this day*.

a month from the month because it is to be celebrated on its festal day.

15/ Now you order the Israelites to celebrate the Passover each year during their generations,[a] once a year on its specific day. Then a pleasing memorial will come[b] before the Lord and no plague will come upon them to kill and to strike (them) during that year when they have celebrated the Passover at its time in every respect as it was commanded.

The Proper Place for Celebrating Passover (49:16–21)

16/ It is not therefore to be eaten outside of the Lord's sanctuary[c] but before the Lord's sanctuary. All the people of the Israelite congregation are to celebrate it at its time. 17/ Every man who has come on its day,[d] who is 20 years of age and above, is to eat it in the sanctuary of your God before the Lord, because this is the way it has been written and ordained— that they are to eat it in the Lord's sanctuary.

18/ When the Israelites enter the land that they will possess—the land of Canaan—and set up the Lord's tabernacle in the middle of the land in one of their tribes, until the time when the Lord's temple will be built in the land, they are to come and celebrate the Passover in the Lord's tabernacle and sacrifice it before the Lord from year to year. 19/ At the time when the house is built in the Lord's name in the land that they will possess, they are to go there and sacrifice the Passover in the evening when the sun sets, in the third part of the day. 20/ They will offer its blood on the base of the altar. They are to place the fat on the fire that is above the altar and are to eat its meat roasted on a fire in the courtyard of the sanctuary in the name of the Lord. 21/ They will not be able to celebrate the Passover in their cities or in any places except before the Lord's tabernacle or otherwise before the house

---

a Lat reads *their generations*, but Eth has *your days/times*.
b Lat has *it will be a pleasing testimony*.
c Lat has *tabernacle*.
d *passes in the census* is the Lat reading (*Jubilees 22–50*, 1169).

in which his name has resided. Then they will not go astray from the Lord.

The Festival of Unleavened Bread (49:22–23)

22/ Now you, Moses, order the Israelites to keep the statute of the Passover as it was commanded to you so that you may tell them its year each year,[a] the time of the days, and the Festival of Unleavened Bread so that they may eat unleavened bread for seven days to celebrate its festival, to bring its sacrifice before the Lord on the altar of your God each day during those seven joyful days. 23/ For you celebrated this festival hastily when you were leaving Egypt until the time you were crossing the sea into the wilderness of Shur, because you completed it on the seashore.

Sabbaths, Weeks, and Jubilees (Chapter 50)

Sabbath Laws in the Wilderness of Sin (50:1)

50:1/ After this law I informed you about the Sabbath days in the wilderness of *Sin*[b] that is between Elim and Sinai.

Sabbaths of Years, Jubilees, and the Chronological System (50:2–5)

2/ On Mount Sinai I told you about the Sabbaths of the land and the years of jubilees in the Sabbaths of the years, but its year we have not told you until the time when you enter the land that you will possess. 3/ The land will observe its Sabbaths when they live on it, and they are to know the year of jubilee. 4/ For this reason I have arranged for you the weeks of years and jubilees—49 jubilees from the time of Adam until today, and one week and two years. It is still 40 years off for learning the Lord's commandments until the time when he leads

---

a Eth reads *its year each year*; Lat has *throughout each and every year*.
b The Eth mss, the only version here, read *Sinai*, a mistake for the similar *Sin*.

(them)[a] across to the land of Canaan, after they have crossed the Jordan to the west of it. 5/ The jubilees will pass by until Israel is pure of every sexual evil, impurity, contamination, sin, and error. Then they will live confidently in the entire land. They will no longer have any satan or any evil one. The land will be pure from that time until eternity.

Sabbath Laws (50:6–13)

6/ I have now written for you the Sabbath commandments and all the statutes of its laws. 7/ You will work for six days, but on the seventh day is the Sabbath of the Lord your God. Do not do any work on it—you, your children, your male and female servants, all your cattle, or the foreigner who is with you. 8/ The person who does any work on it is to die. Any man who desecrates this day; who sleeps with a woman; who says anything about work on it—that he is to set out on a trip on it, or about any selling or buying; who on it draws water that he had not prepared for himself on the sixth day; or who lifts a load to bring (it) outside his tent or his house is to die. 9/ On the Sabbath day do not do any work that you have not prepared for yourself on the sixth day so that you may eat, drink, rest, keep Sabbath on this day from all work, and bless the Lord your God who has given you a festal day and a holy day. This day among their days is to be the day of the holy kingdom for all Israel throughout all time. 10/ For great is the honor that the Lord has given Israel to eat, drink, and be filled on this festal day; and to rest on it from any work that belongs to the work of humanity except to burn incense and to bring before the Lord offerings and sacrifices for the days and Sabbaths. 11/ Only this (kind of) work is to be done on the Sabbath days in the sanctuary of the Lord your God in order that they may atone continuously for Israel with offerings from day to day as a memorial that is acceptable before the Lord; and in order that he may receive them forever, day by day, as you were ordered.

---

a Some Eth copies read *they cross* and others *he crosses*.

12/ Any person who does work: who goes on a trip; who works farmland whether at his home or in any (other) place; who lights a fire; who rides any animal; who travels the sea by ship; any person who beats or kills anything; who slits the throat of an animal or bird; who catches either a wild animal, a bird, or a fish; who fasts and makes war on the Sabbath day—13/ a person who does any of these things on the Sabbath day is to die, so that the Israelites may continue observing the Sabbath in accord with the commandments for the Sabbaths of the land as it was written in the tablets that he placed in my hands so that I could write for you the laws of each specific time in each division of its times.

Postscript

Here the words regarding the divisions of the times are completed.